TAKE YOUR TIME

TAKE
YOUR
TIME

Finding Balance
in a Hurried World

EKNATH EASWARAN

NEW YORK

Copyright © 1994 The Blue Mountain Center of Meditation

Previously published by Nilgiri Press

Library of Congress Cataloging-in-Publication Data

Easwaran, Eknath.
    Take your time : finding balance in a hurried world /
by Eknath Easwaran.—1st ed.
        p.   cm.
    Includes index.
    ISBN 0-7868-6221-1
        1. Time management. 2. Self-management (Psychology)
3. Quality of life. I. Title.
BF637.T5E27   1997
640´.43—dc21   97-3832
                CIP

First Hyperion Edition
10 9 8 7 6 5 4 3 2 1

Table of Contents

Introduction

*T*HIS IS A BOOK about slowing down the pace of life, about taking time for the important things, about living in the present.

Whether you have a demanding job or family responsibilities, whether you are a student or are involved in a creative pursuit, you may feel, like most people, that there is just not enough time in each day. You may feel that you can't take your time, that you cannot slow down the relentless pace of life today. But in my presentation in *Take Your Time* I hope I will be able to show you that you can slow down, and why it is vital that you do so.

Through everyday examples, I will show how we can slow down and be in control even in the midst of pressure, how we can learn not to get caught in automatic responses. The secret lies not in quitting our job or moving to the beach to find tranquility, but in something closer to home.

Step by step we can slow down and train attention to be fully in the present. Then we discover how to free our attention from old patterns in which it has been caught. And, finally, we understand how it is possible to slow down the thinking process itself.

"Living intentionally" is what the Buddha called it, and I will return again and again to this theme. For what I am presenting is a way of life. It begins with the simplest things: making conscious decisions about priorities, for example, and getting up earlier so that we won't begin the day in a rush.

But slowing down is not the goal. It is a means to an end. Living intentionally means being free from cycles of restlessness and inertia, and from automatic responses. Ultimately, it means living at the deepest level of our awareness.

When we begin to slow down, a primary thing becomes clear: doing two or more things at the same time splits our consciousness in two or more ways. So how can we concentrate? How can we feel deeply or think clearly?

When we learn to focus our attention completely in the present, we make an amazing discovery: problems we thought were huge begin to shrink, and old compulsions we thought we could never break out of fall away. We find we have a breathing space between stimulus and response. We no longer blow up when frustrated, because we are going slow enough to control the situation. We no longer cling to a moment of enjoyment, but let things come and go in the natural rhythm of circumstances.

When all our attention is in the present, we find we

have the concentration and the will to make the most of what the day offers. Whether we are rich or poor, young or old, whether we sit behind a desk or drive a bus, whether we are retired or spend our day caring for children, the way of life I am describing opens the possibility of cherishing each day.

In this way of life, we put first things first. We take time for relationships. Especially where children are concerned, we find we can slow down to yield to their rhythm rather than expect them to scurry to keep up with ours.

I introduced the Eight-Point Program described here when I began teaching meditation in the San Francisco Bay Area in the early sixties. As I was privileged to address a growing and diverse circle of people interested in hearing about India's age-old spiritual tradition, I began to give personal instruction in the practice of meditation and the other seven points of the program.

During those turbulent years, many people came to my classes not only to learn to meditate, but to find peace in a troubled world. I found myself being asked questions about the nature of life and happiness. The answers that I gave, I admit, were never original. Whether I answered in terms of having a higher image of the human being or talked about setting a first priority on self-understanding, my words were simply a reinterpretation of enduring spiritual values for a modern audience.

As the years passed, most of the questions stayed the same, but I began to hear a new emphasis. University students became mothers and fathers with demanding jobs. The young people of the sixties who had been concerned about global issues stayed concerned, but now found that they had interests closer to home as well – absorbing careers to pursue, aging parents to cherish, and lively young children to raise. Rather than leaving meditation behind in the tumult of these new activities, an ever-widening circle found the guidance of the Eight-Point Program all the more necessary for finding balance in their hurried world.

Here, in *Take Your Time*, I want to share this same practical, time-tested guidance with my readers. In the seventies, the eighties, and now the nineties, I have continued to teach the same basic program, and although the times have changed and my audience now reaches far beyond California, I have found that these simple practices still work in the same way to open a door to joy and peace.

CHAPTER ONE
Take Your Time

I LEARNED A LESSON in the importance of slowing down during my first Christmas in Berkeley. It was 1960, and I was still new to American ways.

I went down to the post office to send a package to my mother in India. As I neared the sedate old building at the corner of Allston Way and Milvia, erected in a period when the pace of life was slower, I noticed cars double-parked and people darting up and down the broad granite steps. Inside was a scene of frustration, exasperation, and sometimes outright anger.

Crowd or no crowd, I needed to mail my package. I joined a long queue and stood patiently watching the scene around me. I enjoy watching life's passing show, and I have found that there is no need to look for extraordinary situations to find insight and inspiration.

On this occasion, everyone was giving unintended lessons in how to put yourself under pressure. A detached observer would have found the scene amusing. One fellow in front of me was bouncing up and down as if he were on a pogo stick. He was in such a hurry that he just had to release his nervous energy somehow, and with people pressing you in front and behind, the only direction possible is up.

Then I felt a hot breath on the back of my collar. The gentleman in back of me was also in a hurry, and *he* was expending his nervous energy by blowing hot air down my neck.

"Well," I thought, "Christmas is the time for expressions of good will." So I just turned around. "Please take my place," I told him. "I'm not in a hurry."

He was so distracted that he didn't hear me. He just said brusquely, "What?"

"Take my place," I repeated. "I have time. I'm in no hurry at all."

He stared, and then he began to relax. I felt the atmosphere around us begin to change. He apologized for being in such a hurry and mumbled something about being double-parked. I wanted to ask, "Why do you double-park?" But I thought better of it.

Slowly the queue moved forward. The young woman at the counter was probably a college student filling in for the holidays, and she was making mistake after mistake – giving the wrong stamps, giving wrong change – while people complained and corrected her. I could see that she was getting more and more upset; and the more upset she got, the more mistakes she made and the longer each transaction took. All because everybody was in a hurry! If the scene had ever had any Christmas cheer, it was evaporating rapidly.

I'm fond of students; I was a professor for many years. So when it came my turn at the window, I said, "I'm from India. Take your time."

She looked as if she couldn't believe it. But she smiled and relaxed, and she gave me the right change and the right stamps too. I thanked her and wished her a merry Christmas.

As I walked out, I noticed that the man behind me returned her smile. The whole room had relaxed a little; there was even a ripple of laughter at the end of the queue. Pressure is contagious, but so is good will. Just one person slowing down, one person not putting others under pressure, helps everyone else to relax too.

It is not that people are unmannerly or inconsiderate by nature. We just don't have time to be otherwise. If I am rushing to catch the bus, say, and you stand in my way, I don't mean any harm, but I push you aside. This is happening everywhere, every day. People just rush about, and when we rush about we don't see others; they are just phantoms we can pass right through. Then perhaps we say, "Excuse me, beg your pardon, I didn't mean to hurt you." Or perhaps we don't; we're in too much of a hurry. The pace is so fast now that we simply take rudeness, stress, and lack of attention for granted.

This modern civilization of ours has developed a mania for speed. It's a kind of epidemic in which millions of people are caught. And when we become helplessly caught in a universal compulsion, it rarely occurs to us to question whether we are caught, let alone to ask how we can get free.

Almost everyone today complains there is not enough time. What we actually mean is a little different: "not enough time to do everything we want."

Oddly, when we want to do more than we have time for, the first thing we try to get more of every morning is sleep – usually, of course, because we got to bed late from trying to fit more into the night before. So we get up a little late, or just at the last moment, and then hurry through the rest of the day trying to catch up. We rush through breakfast without really seeing what is on the table – if we bother to sit down to a table at all. We barely taste the food or see the faces of those we live with.

So we start the day behind, in a hurry, and of course the pace doesn't stop at home. If anything, it accelerates as the day wears on. We dash for the bus or battle with rush-hour traffic and get to work just barely on time, or even a minute or two late. There is no time to smile and say good morning, no time even to see who's in the office. They are not co-workers; they are specters rushing about and getting in our way.

And in other offices, people are fighting the same pressures. Once I had to go to an unfamiliar, big-city hospital for a minor complaint: I had gone for a swim and had an earache. I was amazed at the scene. Everyone there, staff and patients alike, seemed ready to explode. The staff, overwhelmed by the sheer number of people who needed to be attended to, darted in and out. The patients couldn't dart, of course, but you could see by their faces that they, too, had no time to spend waiting for hours in order to be sent to another room to wait some more. When I was finally ushered into an examination room, the doctor did check both my ears carefully, but I don't think he saw the face between them. He seemed a good man, but he had so little time that I felt he was rather like a highly competent machine, diagnosing another machine. "Faster, faster, faster" means more and more impersonal.

When the day goes like this, by the time evening comes you have been going so fast all day long that you cannot change gears. You have been speeding since you got up; in the evening you whip back home like a boomerang. Not only that, you're *tired*, drained from the pace of it. You drop into a seat on the bus and close your eyes – and just as you do, some mild-mannered chap seated next to you asks innocently, "What is that Australian creature with a three-letter name that ends with a *u*?"

You want to answer politely, but you hear your voice growl, "Emu!" You're thinking, "I don't *care* about crossword puzzles! Who cares about Australian creatures with three-letter names?" You don't think of yourself as a rude person, but your nerves are on edge.

Then, when you reach your stop, you grab your things in such a hurry that you're halfway to the house before you discover that you're carrying somebody else's package. The front gate will not open, and you kick it; then you remember you have a big corn on your toe. By the time you enter your home, you're ready to blow up at the very next person you meet. It's not because you're a cantankerous person. And, just as important, it's not because that's the way life is. This is what speed does to us – to anybody.

★

Constant hurry and day-in, day-out pressure take a cumulative toll on the nervous system. When the hurry becomes chronic, the effects of this toll build up in the mind as well. What begins as nervous tension becomes rigid patterns in the way we think and act. The mind itself gets speeded up; and when the mind gets speeded up, it is easily subject to negative emotions like anger and fear. A racing mind is simply moving too fast for love, compassion, tenderness, and similarly quiet states. Judgment is replaced by snap decisions. In a mad rush, in a frantic hurry, where is the time for making choices?

On the hairpin curves in the hills around the Bay Area there are signs warning "25 miles per hour." It reminds me of the Blue Mountain area of South India where I used to live. On those winding, narrow roads there was one dangerous hairpin curve after another. But since many drivers did not know how to read, instead of a sign saying "25 miles per hour" there was a grisly picture of a human skull. Most drivers immediately became cautious when they saw that skull, because a mistake on those roads could be fatal.

Every driver understands that if you go too fast, you can't control your car. But few of us understand that the mind is very much like a car. It drives us through life, and we go where it takes us. When we are in a hurry, the mind is moving too fast for us to absorb what is going on around us, heed the warning signs, and make the judgment calls we need to avoid a potential accident. And when judgment is blurred by speed, we are in the greatest danger. It is no exaggeration to say that we are then on a mountain road taking blind hairpin bends at sixty miles an hour, barely holding the road.

"Living in the fast lane" has become a notorious phrase with reason. Nobody should travel in that fast lane. When your life and your mind are going faster and faster, there *can* be no decisions. There are only reflexes – and reflexes become compulsive. When the same thought – that is, the same emotional response, the same urge, the same craving – repeats itself over and over again without a break, it becomes compulsive. It can be a compulsive addiction to smoking or drugs, it can be a compulsive attachment to a particular person: whatever it is, every compulsive cycle of thinking is dangerous because it means we are not free. The mind is as powerful as a Ferrari. We cannot get control of our behavior until we get a firm grip on the wheel. And that means we have to learn to slow down our pace of living.

★

Those of you who have been born and brought up in this country are probably not aware of how unnecessarily, how uncomfortably speeded up we have made our lives. But there are a few signs – as simple as the grisly skull and crossbones of the Indian roadside – to warn us that our whole society is careening out of control in the fast lane of life.

One sure sign is that no one seems to have enough time. A second is that people are almost always hurrying to be late. And third, it seems as if everyone is trying to fit more and more into the same fixed twenty-four hours of day and night, less and less satisfied with what time offers them. That is the paradox: we hurry faster and faster only to find we have less and less time.

Have you ever noticed that when you try to fit more and more into a day, you're likely to go through the whole day late? Trying to squeeze more in, we only squeeze time out. We have forgotten that it is possible to go through the day slowly and carefully, tending to each matter as it comes up but always keeping a sense of priorities.

People who are in control of their lives somehow manage to be on time without arriving hurried. They get things done without even getting flustered about it, while the rest of us, constantly harried by the pressures of life, go from place to place always just a little late and slightly unprepared.

I have had the privilege of seeing one person who was a real master of pressures and priorities. Mahatma Gandhi has been an ideal for me since I met him when I was a college student in the early thirties. Gandhi was constantly under pressure, but it never seemed to touch

him. At the height of India's revolution for independence from British rule, I have seen him go into an
emergency meeting with the country's top leaders and
come out hours later looking as if he had been playing
bingo all day.

Unlike the vast majority of the rest of us in India,
Gandhi considered it a mark not only of courtesy but of
mastery to be on time wherever he went. Time was precious to him, other people were precious to him, so he
treated their time and his own with the utmost respect.
He wore only one piece of cloth around his waist and a
second around his shoulders, but there was always a
large pocket watch pinned to his garment with a safety
pin. It was one of his noted eccentricities. And if anyone
was late for an appointment with him, he would take
this watch up and show it to him, even if the visitor happened to be someone very distinguished. That was his
gentle way of teaching us to learn to be on time – because, as you know, we Indians have a not undeserved
reputation for not taking punctuality too seriously.

In fact, there are many stories told at our expense
about the annoying indifference to time in my old country. One story tells of some Western tourists who were
waiting in Madras Central Station to catch a train to
North India. The train is called the Grand Trunk Express, and long ago a British wit observed that it was
neither grand nor trunk nor an express. Its reputation
for a cavalier approach to schedules had spread far and
wide. So these tourists had been warned they might
have to wait for hours. To their amazement, the Grand

Trunk Express steamed in right on time. They boarded, sought out the guard, and apologized for the calumny that had been spreading about his train. He smiled. "Thank you very much for your appreciation," he replied, "but I have to tell you this is last evening's train."

Lack of punctuality is not confined to the easygoing East, however. It is common in the efficient West as well. When I go to the theater, for example, I notice how often people come in late. My wife, Christine, and I used to go to the theater frequently, and we are real theater buffs. We like to show up in good time, take our seats in advance of the crowd, and enjoy the sense of pleasant anticipation while waiting for the play to begin.

About five minutes or so before curtain time, people begin to stream in. In theaters, of course, leg room is at a premium. It's like sitting in a jet. Every time someone wants to get by, you have to twist your legs and then untwist them again, which gets to be a real bother. And even after the play has started, there will usually be latecomers. After all, there are traffic jams and parking problems, and people have to go back to get their keys. So there are always a few who need to climb in over you, each asking, "Excuse me, may I pass?" You try to handle the situation by contracting yourself into someone so thin that he doesn't take up any space at all; but there is nowhere to put your legs, so the latecomers unerringly step on your toes – all while the opening lines are being declaimed on stage.

Being a few minutes late seems minor. But arriving

late over and over again, whether it is to a play or to a business meeting or to an appointment at home, cannot help but create stress. We're constantly arriving just a little out of breath and unprepared, needing a few more minutes to catch up and get "up to speed again" in our new situation. Again, we're actually losing time – and usually, again, from trying to squeeze more in. The stress accumulates, and the lost time adds up as the day goes on.

Not only that, being late adds to the stress of others too – those who own the toes we step on. When everyone arrives on time, nobody gets disturbed. Another unnecessary pinprick of agitation is avoided, to the benefit of everyone around.

★

Today, because of the fast pace of life, the word *stress* has become a part of our everyday vocabulary.

When I first came to this country, only a few occupations were considered "high stress." Today everybody is under stress. We enroll in courses for reducing stress, read books and articles about it, and even watch television programs advising us how to eliminate it from our lives. If we could do this, we would be eliminating life itself. Life *is* full of stress, and stress does need to be managed: but not by eliminating it. The key to managing stress is to make ourselves stress-resistant, and that begins with slowing down the hurried pace of our lives.

Since I am a meditation teacher, people often ask me

if meditation can help them avoid stress. I always advise them, "Don't try to avoid stress. The more you avoid it, the more it'll come your way. Instead, tell life, 'I am not afraid of you. I am not going to ask for any favors. Give me whatever you want; I can make the best of it.'"

Oddly, when you can truly say to life, "I don't care what you bring me," life has a curious way of treating you with respect and saying, "Yes, ma'am. Yes, sir. Anything you like."

The problems of life are not really "out there"; they are "in here." Everything is decided in and by the mind. However capable a person is, if he believes he cannot cope with a particular situation, he is likely to prove as inadequate as he feels. The person who thinks she is unequal to a challenge will probably never succeed in meeting it. This kind of negative thinking can slowly make it impossible for anyone to function adequately.

It is by acting as if we were equal to any challenge and meeting challenges over and over again that we get the skill to cope with any situation that comes our way. Challenges need not be hard on our health: in fact, I would go to the extent of saying that challenges can be good for our health, because by meeting challenges we gain a kind of hardiness which helps even in resisting disease. With this kind of hardiness, we do not simply survive stress but flourish on it.

Gandhi once made a revealing confession: "I love storms." Trials and tribulations brought out the best in him. This can be true even of ordinary people like you and me. I actually feel good when the storms of life are coming – and although I don't talk about it much, my weather is mostly stormy.

Just as we have waterproof clothes to wear when we go out in the rain, when we go into stormy weather in life we need to stress-proof the mind. The opposite kind of person is the one who feels helpless: who believes that everything is decided outside, that external circumstances dictate to him how to behave.

A mind that is racing over worries about the future or recycling resentments from the past is ill equipped to handle the challenges of the moment. By slowing down, we can train the mind to focus completely in the present. Then we will find that we can function well whatever the difficulties. That is what it means to be stress-proof: not avoiding stress but being at our best under pressure, calm, cool, and creative in the midst of the storm.

★

Friends in this country sometimes tell me, "I know all this rushing around is not good for me, but I've got to hurry to get things done. I have to do two or more things at once to accomplish what I want as well as what is required of me. After all, I do want to live a full life."

I reply, "It is a superstition to think that you have to hurry."

A slower life is not an ineffective life; it is not an unartistic life; it is not a boring life. Just the opposite. It is much more effective, much more artistic, much richer than a life lived as a race against the clock. It gives you time to pause, to think, to reflect, to decide, to weigh pros and cons. It gives you time for relationships.

The problems of modern life aren't insoluble. We needn't accept a life of hurry, disharmony, and violence. We needn't accept a life in which we are pushed and pulled by forces beyond our control. Not too long ago, in many areas of the world, people led simple, beautiful lives.

I recall rather nostalgically the beautiful village in which I grew up. My home state of Kerala is a green staircase on the southwest coast of India. Visitors from the West are often surprised at the beauty of the whole state, and amazed at the independent, hardworking, contented, simple way of life which the people there are still able to follow in spite of many difficulties.

When I was growing up, my village was rather backward according to modern Western standards. There was no electricity; there was no cinema; there was no radio; there were no police; there was no court of law. People have said to me on occasion, "It must have been a rather uninteresting life." I reply, "Just the opposite."

The air was pure, the water pure; rainfall was abundant and the soil fertile. My area was surplus-producing farmland. Everything we needed was grown in or near our village. We had no need for big trucks to bring in things from outside, or big highways to provide access. We didn't transport goods: we grew everything, produced everything ourselves. We grew cereals, vegetables, and fruits; we grew the coconuts that supplied us not only with food but with fiber for ropes and oil which was extracted right in the village. All the craftsmen we needed – carpenters, blacksmiths, goldsmiths, potters, weavers – lived there in the village too.

Don't get the impression that this was a rustic life without artistry or beauty. I received an excellent education in our little village school, where several of my teachers were my uncles. And I received a different kind of education from the land itself. For entertainment, we had the best classical Indian music. One of my uncles was an accomplished musician who had trained his family into an ensemble, and we had concerts often. For theater we had Kathakali, an ancient dance form famous today all over the world, depicting wonderful stories from the great Indian epics *Ramayana* and *Mahabharata*. In my family we put on our own plays too, with a traditional or religious theme. I'll never forget the night I played the god of fire, a minor character in a romance. To show that I was an immortal rather than a mere mortal, I had to sit on a chair so that my feet would not touch the floor. And I had to keep my eyes from blinking, which is harder than it sounds.

People in my village were subject to the usual human foibles and discontents, of course. But we were all much more contented than I find people are today in our vastly more affluent society. The pressures of the consumer society that we take for granted here simply did not exist in those days in my village. For example, even people with a lot of money and prestige dressed very simply. On special occasions, the women of my ancestral family would just go to the almirah and select sumptuous silk saris with gold borders, and in a few minutes they were dressed for the most formal occasion. The sari is a simple, seamless garment, but I don't think any other costume can rival it for elegance and grace. For us men, it was even simpler: all we had to do was don a plain white shirt over the dhoti, which covers the lower body, to be presentable at any affair. This is true in India, I think, even today. Years after I had left my village, I took a friend to visit a lawyer in Madras. The lawyer excused himself, saying, "May I go and dress?" He was gone only a moment, because all he had to do was put on a shirt to cover his bare chest.

Of course, in our village we didn't have any cars; we all walked. The roads were lined with mango and banyan trees where we could see monkeys playing. Walking was not a chore; it was a source of simple delight. A few in the village had bicycles – in fact, I can still remember the first time a bicycle appeared in the village, when my father pedaled into our family compound.

In my case, I didn't walk to school; I ran. My school was a mile away, and I had about an hour for my lunch break, so I used to run home, just to have my lunch from my granny's hands, and then run back again. We didn't have clocks, either; my granny would tell me that it was time for school when she saw the sun reach the middle of the veranda. So even clocks and cars are not strictly necessary to get an education.

Please don't misunderstand me. I am not suggesting that we all move to Kerala or Molokai to live simple, quiet lives. I know this is not possible, nor is it desirable. Each of us has a contribution to make to the world, and I am not suggesting that we run away from our problems and opportunities. Neither am I suggesting that we return to the kind of lives our grandfathers and grandmothers lived. Yet I know that there was much beauty and much wisdom in their slower way of life, even though they did not have all of the modern conveniences we enjoy.

In my sixteenth year – the customary age in India to finish high school in those days – I left my village to go to college. Like most healthy teenagers, I quickly abandoned my village ways, immersing myself wholeheartedly in the Western influences which the British had brought to India. Only after many years did I begin to see that in moving beyond a narrow, village outlook, I had thrown out much that was beneficial too. After my grandmother died, I turned to meditation and began to look for ways to blend the very best of Western culture and my own Indian heritage into a way of life truly suited for the hectic modern world.

Even in India this was a challenge. My life as a professor of English literature was busy from early morning until late at night with all kinds of pressures. But I hadn't seen anything until I came to this country on the Fulbright exchange program in 1959.

The moment I disembarked from the *Queen Elizabeth*

in New York City, I was surrounded by a ceaseless stream of traffic – a bewildering display of speed and noise. Nothing had prepared me for that sight. My first impression was of millions of cars flashing by. I thought there must be some mammoth race going on, with people racing for their very lives.

I could not understand why all these cars were rushing about like that. Naturally, I took it for granted that once the sun set, the scene would quiet down; all those people would finally get wherever they were in such a hurry to get to and stagger out of their vehicles for a little rest. There I had my second shock: the traffic continued even after the sun had set. I had thought the peace and quiet of evening would set the cars at rest. The peace and quiet never came. Eight o'clock came, then nine o'clock, then ten . . . the traffic just went on and on. What seemed completely unnatural to me had become, to the people of New York, a way of life.

That very first day I made a conscious decision never to get caught in that fast lane.

Friends told me, "The pace of life here *is* fast. You'll just have to adjust to it. You *will* adjust to it, given time." I replied, "I don't want to enter that race – and not only that, I would like to show you how to slow down, too."

That was in 1959. I have lived in this country for over thirty years now, and I have kept my resolve. Not once have I got speeded up by the pace of life here, no matter how severe the pressures around me. And I am proud to say that in those thirty years I have helped probably thousands of people to slow down too. From that experience has come this book.

★

One of the first things I discovered – long before I even came to New York – is that it isn't necessary to lead a frantic life to accomplish many things.

Again, I had the living example of Gandhi. Very, very few people in human history have accomplished more than Gandhi. Not many people even have the colossal vitality he had. But he generally looked so relaxed that a superficial observer might have thought he was lazy. If you look at some of the pictures of Gandhi, he looks so relaxed that he reminds me of our cat. Our cat just sits quietly at the foot of a tree, so restful that you think she is sleeping. Then, without any warning, you see a blur of half a dozen cats in the air. Such an explosion of movement! I always wonder where all this energy comes from. To look at her, she seems absolutely static; but when in action, she becomes not just one cat but half a dozen.

Gandhi was like that. When you looked at him, he looked so quiet, so gentle, so mild, that it took a long time for the British to understand that just as a cat becomes half a dozen cats in the air, Gandhi became four hundred million human beings when he stirred the unconscious aspirations of the Indian people.

This is just the opposite of the so-called Type A personality, always on the go in an obsessive drive to achieve more and more in less and less time. Gandhi represents the real Type B, the spiritual type, calm at the center but able to rouse a whirlwind of selfless action when the occasion demands. From the outside, such a person may look like an old Model T, but inside there is a Ferrari. Gandhi was a Model T with a Ferrari engine. How often we find people the other way around! A Ferrari body with a Model T engine inside. You see a lot of speed and flash but not a lot of real progress, and no lasting contribution to the world.

Actually, although Gandhi looks frail in photographs, he had not only a Ferrari engine but a Ferrari body as well. Only a strong, resilient body could have taken the rigors of that life. John Gunther, who was over six feet tall, recalled that he had to run to keep up with Gandhi when he went to interview him – and Gandhi was in his seventies at the time. His vigor was unmistakable. His power was untouched until the situation demanded it; then he would take off in no time, from zero to sixty in one minute, as calm as ever behind the wheel. It was all power steering, too – just the opposite of the stereotype of the tense, time-driven man of action. I was only a student when I met him, and it gave me a whole new ideal of what it means to operate successfully in the modern world.

Even little incidents in Gandhi's life were a lesson to me, and Gandhi as a public speaker was an inspiration. I read somewhere that, in a recent poll, fear of public speaking ranked highest on people's lists of what they found most stressful, even higher than death, divorce and taxes. I can sympathize easily. I was keenly interested in public speaking as a college student, but when I had to stand before an audience in the early days, my limbs would shake and the words would choke in my throat. It encouraged me greatly to learn that as a student, Gandhi too had been so acutely shy that he was unable even to read a prepared, brief introduction at a dinner party. Of course, he not only learned to overcome this shyness but spoke every day for most of his public life, often before some of the biggest and most hostile crowds you can imagine. But he was always relaxed and free from tension. There was no hurry, and he never succumbed to pressure.

One amusing instance of this has been preserved in the archives of radio. When Gandhi was in London in 1931 as a guest of the British government, he had become something of a celebrity in the United States, and CBS arranged a special transatlantic broadcast – a daring feat of technology in those days – so that people in this country could hear him speak. Everything was set up hours beforehand, and the radio and government people were all tense and under pressure, because in those days a radio link on this scale was delicate and expensive, and a live broadcast from England to America was rare. Most of Gandhi's entourage was getting flustered too. A lot was at stake. It was important to them that Gandhi be effective in conveying his message to this large and influential audience.

Gandhi himself, however, didn't have any preparations to make. He had nothing to do with the arrangements; all he was expected to do was move the hearts of several million people in their native language when the time came. So he conducted his regular affairs in the midst of the confusion, waiting for his cue.

Finally a harassed-looking executive came over and said urgently, "Mr. Gandhi, the radio is ready for you. They are waiting in America!"

Gandhi sat down in front of the microphone and said, "You want me to speak into this?" Millions of people heard him, because he was already on the air. Everyone laughed as the speakers broadcast his words back into the room. The tension was broken, and Gandhi began to speak impromptu – with complete concentration, in no hurry, with total mastery of himself and the situation. You can still listen to the recording of that broadcast. It is one of the most moving speeches I have ever heard.

★

When I present the picture of the slow, fulfilled life, I am presenting life at its best – physically, mentally, intellectually, and of course spiritually. To make this way of life a reality, I have adapted a set of eight universal techniques to fit into our modern way of life. I know that this program can be practiced in the midst of an active, full life because I did so myself while working hard at a great university in India. The only adjustment I made in this program when I began to teach it to others in this country was to place more emphasis on slowing down.

This Eight-Point Program consists of the following steps: slowing down, one-pointed attention, training the senses, putting others first, spiritual companionship, spiritual reading, repetition of a mantram, and meditation.

Although I am a teacher of meditation, I have not written this book for people who want to learn to meditate (though instructions in meditation are included in the seventh chapter). I have written it for those who want to get the most from life by gaining freedom from the forces that hurry and hassle them through each day. The Buddha called this ideal "intentional living." It is the opposite of reflex living, which is scarcely living at all.

Over many years, I have found that for most of us the first step toward living intentionally is to slow down. By slowing down and getting hold of our attention, we gain the capacity to make wise choices every day – choices of how we use our time, of where we place our resources and our love. I am not just talking about avoiding what you call "the rat race." I am talking about a life full of an artistic beauty that has almost vanished from modern civilization, but is quite within the reach of everyone.

By living intentionally, I believe, we do more than simply elevate our own personal lives. We begin to remake our civilization. We can begin to transform our global jungle into a real global village, where our children will remember naturally the needs of all the children on the face of the earth. This is our destiny. This is what we were all born for and what we have been looking for all of our lives, whatever else we have been seeking.

CHAPTER TWO
Slowing Down

V ERY WELL, we need to slow down. But how?

To paraphrase the Buddha, we learn to slow down by trying to slow down. In this chapter I shall give some ways to start – ways I myself used in the often hectic days of my university teaching career. The suggestions that follow are not "quick fixes" – tricks you have only to do once to get more time for the rest of your life. They are skills and grow through practice. The more you apply them, the more opportunities you will find to apply them further. Even today, after decades, I am still fine-tuning the ways in which I spend my time each day – finding new adjustments I can make to give me a little more time for what matters to me most.

1. Get Up Early

The easiest way to get more time is so simple that many people overlook it: get up early.

Getting up early does much more than simply

gain another hour or so of clock time. The pace you set first thing in the morning is likely to stay with you through the day, so if you get up early and set a calm, unfrenzied pace, you are much less likely to get speeded up later on as the pressures of the day close in on you.

Actually, I would suggest that you not only get up early but set aside half an hour first thing every morning – perhaps after your shower or tea – for meditation or inspiring reading, instead of plunging headlong into what you have to do.

This simple step has profound effects. In the natural rhythms of life, there is a period in the junctions between night and day, in the ebb and flow between activity and rest, when the mind grows calm. If you set aside a period of quiet time early in the morning, it puts your activities into a longer perspective which will stay with you all day. (I shall be saying more about this later, because both meditation and inspiring reading are part of my Eight-Point Program.)

Then, if at all possible, have a leisurely breakfast with family or friends before going off to work or school. If you live alone, it is still helpful to sit down with a nourishing breakfast – don't eat it standing up! – and enjoy it without hurry. All these things set the pace you will be following for the rest of the day – and, to the extent they become habits, for the rest of your life.

Similarly, get to work a little early – in time to get to your desk without crashing through the office, in time to speak to the janitor and your co-workers, in time for a few minutes of reflection while you arrange the prior ities that face you at work. These are simple steps, but they can go a long way in slowing down the pace of life, not only for you but for those around you as well.

There is a quiet joy in getting up early that people seem to have forgotten. In some circles, getting up early is out of fashion. In Berkeley, when the ways of sophisticated students were still new to me, I once phoned a graduate student around nine or nine-thirty in the morning. After a long pause somebody picked up the telephone, and I heard a muffled noise at the other end. I said, "Hello."

"I'm not awake," the voice of my friend growled. "Call me later." Then he hung up. He was appalled later when he discovered who his caller had been. By way of apology he tried to explain, "You don't know Berkeley."

That was true. Students in Berkeley used to tell me candidly, "We have heard about the beauty of the sunrise, but personally we haven't experienced it." They were bright students, but they hadn't realized that by going to bed late and getting up late they were not exactly living in harmony with the rhythms of life.

The usual student excuse is, "I went to bed late, so how can you expect me to get up early?" Or, for those who don't really need an excuse, "What does it matter?" It actually matters quite a bit, because it determines the pace of the whole day. The earlier you get up in the morning, the better start you get in life.

At the University of Minnesota I used to go to the cafeteria at seven-thirty, when it opened, and sit down to enjoy a leisurely breakfast. At about ten to eight all the doors would burst open, and the scholars of Minnesota would come pouring in by the hundreds, sweeping through the cafeteria line reaching out for food like those Hindu gods and goddesses with many arms. They would alight briefly at the table, inhale their food, and in ten minutes they would all be gone – because most of them had eight o'clock classes. It never failed to astound me.

Finally, one morning I stopped a student I knew and asked him, "Tell me, why do you come at ten to eight?"

He was really embarrassed at my simplicity. "Because," he explained, "I get up at a quarter to eight."

This is how many people begin their day, whether they are going to school or going to work, and it means they are going to rush from place to place all day long.

2. Don't Crowd Your Day

The desire to fit more and more into a given span of time is pervasive, and technology has merely added to the pressure. We are expected to keep up with more and more information at work and at home, and the media obligingly drown us in it. New technologies offer to help us sort out what is important from what is trivial, but not to tell which of it, if any, really *is* important and how to get the time to evaluate it – while all the time they drown us in more. I know many people who feel duty-bound to keep up with all of it, too. After all, the TV and newspapers and magazines *are* there, so we really ought to know what's in them . . .

Quite a few people, I imagine, subscribe to more

periodicals than they read. It is a rare person who doesn't have at least one small pile of magazines in the corner waiting to be scanned before they are tossed, perhaps dating back months or even years. Once, impressed by the stack I saw in the home of a friend, I observed naively, "I didn't know there *were* that many periodicals about travel."

"Oh," he assured me, "I don't even get all there are. I used to subscribe to more, but I finally dropped them."

I knew he had heavy family and job responsibilities, so I asked, "How do you find time to read them all?"

"I don't actually read them all," he admitted. "But my wife and I look forward to our two weeks of vacation in August, and we want to be sure we find the right destination. I guess you could say travel is our hobby. So we try to stay informed."

And this was only his hobby. What if he had been a travel agent? He probably would have had five times as many publications lying on his desk, waiting to be read.

Or take newspapers. To be well informed, we take it for granted that we have to read at least one daily paper, and perhaps some weekly news magazines as well. But look at the investment of time that is required just to read the Sunday edition of the *New York Times*!

Of course, for many people the answer is to try speed reading. I first encountered this phrase in 1959 – in this country, of course – and having lived in the world of books for most of my life, I was immediately skeptical.

In those days, proponents of speed reading boasted that it would enable you to read *War and Peace* in a few hours. One columnist I read admitted that she had been able to do it, too, but that afterwards all she could remember was that it had something to do with war between Russia and France. As a professor of literature, I wouldn't have given that kind of observation very high marks.

Many other teachers felt the same way, of course, and I don't think speed reading was taken seriously for long in the world of education. But I still hear it touted as an answer for busy executives and professionals, as well as for ordinary people like you and me trying not to drown in the wash of information around us. Here, it is argued, not much is lost if you miss a lot of content. The point is simply to get through what the mail brings before the next batch arrives. It is a race – like so much else in our lives. But do we really want to be in it?

The obvious answer to this dilemma is, If things are not worth reading, why should we read them? When we feel we're being robbed of precious time already, do we really want to spend it on what only adds to the noise and clutter in the mind? And most of these newspapers and magazines are a sad waste of trees as well.

I grew up appreciating Carlyle's statement that "a good book is the purest essence of a human soul." I have always loved to read. But even as a student I would seek out something truly worth reading and read it slowly, with concentration, so as to absorb all the author had poured into it.

I say this as a real bookworm. Books were rare in India when I was young, and in the small Catholic college in South India I attended, every new book was precious. Occasionally the pages had to be cut open by hand, an act I treated with reverence; and the smell of fresh ink on paper was perfume for me, like Chanel No.5.

My college library was quite small by American standards, but to me it was a treasury. I knew every inch of the shelves as well as the librarian himself – his name was John – and his only assistant, whose name was Anthony. (Names like John and Anthony were not unusual for Indian boys in a Catholic college.) There was no elaborate catalog system; when new books came in, John often just stuck them in wherever there was space on the shelf. And that is how I came to seal my reputation as a bookworm.

One afternoon, as it happened, some member of the faculty had asked for a particular book that was not usually in demand. Anthony did not know how to find it and neither did John. Finally Anthony came rushing into the class I was attending, called me out, and asked, "Can you find this book that so-and-so wants? I need it immediately."

I went to the library, went straight up the ladder, took the book, and put it in his hands. He was suitably impressed. "Thank you," he said sincerely. "You have saved my honor."

It led to an undeserved reputation as a scholar. But really I was just a reader – a reader who ranged wide but who always went deep. I just couldn't see a reason for reading any other way.

This seems to me all the more important with the

abundance of reading material that surrounds us in this affluent, literate country. I marvel at the number of books and magazines I find even in a supermarket. But when I look at their covers, I almost envy my grandmother her illiteracy.

Make wise choices about what you read: read only what is worthwhile. And then take the time to read carefully. I like to read slowly and with complete attention; I don't even like background music or a cup of coffee at my side. And when I reach the end of a chapter or a section, I close the book and reflect on what I have read. I would much rather read one good book with concentration and understanding than to skim through a list of best-sellers which I will not remember and which will have no effect on my life or my understanding of life. One book read with concentration and reflected upon is worth a hundred books flashed through without any absorption at all.

A well-educated friend once told me that she often reads ten or twenty things at a time. "Really?" I asked. I was amazed.

"Oh," she explained, "not *literally*. But at any given time, I'm likely to be in the middle of reading that many.

"Actually," she added, "I really don't finish most of them, either. I get about halfway through, and then I find something else I want to read instead. But I never quite admit to myself that I'm not going to return to that book and finish it. So it sits in my 'to-be-read' pile."

This is a rather common phenomenon, and I think it is usually just another expression of wanting to "do it all." But it reveals one more deleterious side effect of a speeded-up life: a shortened attention span. People whose span of attention is short find it difficult to finish a book, or even to sit through a movie. I know a man who would go to a multiplex theater and move from room to room, watching parts of three or more movies in the time it would take to sit through one. He couldn't sit still through any one film because there was not enough action on the screen to keep him in his seat.

We see this most with television, of course. Even a half-hour program seems to stretch our diminishing capacity to pay attention. "Channel surfing" has replaced watching a complete show. I admit that I, too, would not find anything in most of these programs to hold my attention. But once we have learned there is nothing worth watching, why not turn it off? Flitting through fifty or more channels is going to divide our attention even more. And when we can't get our mind to slow down enough to stay on the same focus, how can we expect to enjoy anything? How can we do a good job at anything we do?

Of course, this is a vicious circle. When TV producers know they have, say, fifteen seconds to engage our attention, they reduce it to ten. Ten seconds maximum for staying with any given thought, idea, or emotion! But otherwise they fear they will lose their audience. Commercials and children's programs, in particular, have a pace and intensity that assumes ten seconds is eternity.

Because our lives are so fast, a short attention span is often taken for granted. I have even heard people brag about how short their attention is, as if that were a sign of creative ferment. Actually, it is only one more long-term effect of trying to fit everything into less and less time. A truly creative mind has a very *long* attention span. When a great painter, musician, or scientist turns to a subject, he or she stays with it not for minutes but for hours, days, and even years, going deeper and deeper.

The way to break this cycle of shorter and shorter attention is simply to stop trying to do everything possible. To slow down, it is important to realize that we can't read everything, can't keep ourselves entertained at the maximum every available moment, can't absorb or even catch all the so-called information that is offered to us every day. We have to make choices. And with the "information highway" on the horizon, I would add, the need to make these kinds of choices is only going to get more pressing.

It's not only with ourselves that we try to squeeze more and more into our lives. We do so with the lives of those we love as well.

I know many parents, for example, who spend a great deal of time ferrying children to after-school activities. I am all for giving children opportunities, but even here we need to be selective – perhaps especially here, because children have little control of their own time. Their time is in our hands.

Many parents today think children are deprived if they do not have a variety of activities. But this simply isn't so. Children are deprived if they don't have their parents' love and attention, they are deprived if they don't have food and fresh air and a good education and time for play, but they really lose very little if they are not always moving from scout meeting to soccer practice to piano lessons to karate. Even more than adults, children need to be protected from the pressure to hurry. When we fill their days with endeavors – often, of course, to fulfill some childhood desire of our own – we are only teaching them to hurry, hurry, hurry as we do.

Because of the pressures of what is considered to be a full life, parents often find themselves taking their children to soccer practice one day, dance class the next, a birthday party the third, and a shopping trip the fourth. Even high school students may not need this kind of schedule to absorb their energy, but here I am talking about children who haven't reached their teens.

Greater pressures await if the child does not come up to parents' expectations in school. Then after-school tutoring, counseling, and psychologists become an absolute necessity. Wanting our children to have every advantage, we never ask, "Is all this rushing around good for Bobby? Is this constant pressure really helping Susan?"

Few families today are wealthy. They have to make financial sacrifices to see that their children receive all this extracurricular instruction. So the financial pressures build up as well as the pressures of time.

3. Ask "What Is Important?"

Long ago, when I began to see how much meditation offered, I wanted to make sure I took time for it every day. But I couldn't see how I could fit it in. I had an extremely busy schedule, with responsibilities from early morning until late at night, when students used to come for help with their studies while I was reading or writing or preparing for the next day's classes.

I valued all of this, but I was determined to make meditation a top priority. So I finally sat down and made a list of all the things I felt bound to do.

Then I took my red pencil and crossed out everything that was not necessary or actually beneficial. There were some surprising results. I found I had been involved in activities that I couldn't honestly say benefited anyone, including myself. I had simply enjoyed doing them.

When I surveyed what remained, I found I had freed a number of hours every week.

It is somewhat painful to do this, I admit. But very quickly you will find it liberating. You will find you have more time to do the things that are important to you, more time for family and friends, more time for those periods of reflection – and for meditation, which I will be presenting later in the book – which make life worthwhile.

Of course, this list reflects *your* priorities, no one else's. No one will be looking over your shoulder while you decide what gets the red pencil. And, of course, the list is not permanent. Every now and then I still repeat this exercise, making a list and questioning all my activities because priorities change.

One of the most important things about this kind of review is that it is an admission to yourself that you can't do everything. Once you make this realization, you can begin to ask, "What do I want to do? What is important?" When all is said and done, if you don't make this list for yourself, the pressures of everyday life will simply make it for you.

To get a fresh perspective on activities you may be engaged in simply out of habit, or other reasons that masquerade as necessity, you may find it helpful to show your list to a detached friend. However, very, very few people have this kind of detachment, for it requires that they not get personally involved. Another way to evaluate your activities is to ask yourself, "Will this help the next generation?"

When you have pared down your list, test your decision for a few weeks. Very often you will find that you and the world can do without activities you had thought essential, and that you have all kinds of new time to allocate as you choose.

When I first made this kind of list, I found to my surprise that quite a few of the things I had been engaged in were expendable. I had never suspected this. I had become used to certain activities that university professors do; and then, too, I had taken it for granted that other activities really could not manage without my contribution.

For one thing, I was associated with a number of little academic clubs: a current events club, the dramatic society, the debating society, a club for the study of obscure English poets . . . I even had a central role with the Toastmaster's Club at the YMCA. When I dropped out of these activities, I was under the impression that people would miss me. I even asked myself what I would do when people asked why I hadn't been turning up. I was rather embarrassed to discover that nobody noticed my absence. Nobody even asked, "Where have you been?" It was a very healthy reminder.

So even if you can't imagine how the team will do without your coaching skills next year, or how the neighborhood children will get to their swimming lessons without your van, I can assure you that it's very likely that others will arise to carry the burden. They may even have been looking forward to the opportunity to try.

4. Take Time for Relationships

When you are trying to slow down, it is important to take time for personal relationships, which are usually the first casualties in a speeded-up way of life.

This may sound like odd advice: I have just suggested spending less time on superfluous activities, and now I'm saying to give more time to others. And it is true that relationships require time – sometimes a good deal of time. But it is time well spent.

Take the simple question of meals. As the pace of life has accelerated, a great many of us have got out of the habit of sitting together and sharing a leisurely meal with family or friends. Often we eat alone, in a hurry, on our feet, even on the run or behind the wheel. I know people who seldom really eat a meal at all; they forage, or string together a series of snacks. This is not only the result of hurry, it adds to it. We can slow down by taking the time – *making* the time – to find a friend or two and create a little oasis in our day where we can shut out the pressures around us and enjoy human company.

This is especially important for a family – and vital for those with children. Shared meals form a bond that keeps the family together. But family meals have lost their importance today because everyone is in a hurry. It is a rare occasion to sit together and enjoy a meal, as most families used to do every day.

Eating together is considered a sacrament in many cultures. These simple bonds play a part in holding a society together. So even if you live alone, arrange to share a meal regularly with friends or family. I know people who live alone through choice, but who carefully maintain and nurture personal relationships by getting together with friends to prepare and enjoy meals. It is not only nutrition you are getting when you do this, but also the loving companionship shared by everyone at the table.

Personal relationships, of course, not only take time, they take "quality time." This is especially true in relationships with children, where what matters is not so much the number of hours we spend as the attention we give, the love we show, the extent to which we enter into the child's world instead of dragging him or her into our own.

Every child needs the companionship of mom and dad. But mom and dad have to slow down in order to go at the child's pace. When I go to a shopping center, I often see little children being dragged from place to place crying their heads off while their parents get more and more impatient and agitated. They are in a hurry, for reasons which to them are clear and legitimate. But the children don't understand, and crying is the only language that small children know. They can't express themselves any differently. It is up to us to take time to understand their needs.

Children, as most sensitive parents know, cannot reasonably be kept to a schedule. Schedules are fine at the office, but young children have a sense of time that is very different – and much more natural. They don't know about appointments and parking meters and living in the fast lane, and we cannot make them understand; all we can do is hurry them along. It is we adults who must learn to slow down enough to enter their world, not their job to speed up and join ours.

To me it is tragic to try to accelerate a child's development so that he or she can enter the adult world. Where is the hurry? What period of life is more precious than childhood? If we understood its worth, we would devote ourselves to slowing down the pace of childhood instead of rushing our children out of it. As Wordsworth said, "Heaven lies about us in our infancy!"

Just as we try to fill our children's lives with worthwhile activities, we try to fill them up with gifts. But children need time more than toys. In fact, our time is what they all want most.

I read not long ago that greeting card companies are beginning to exploit the sensitivities of parents on the go, with cards that can be tucked under the box of cereal on the table: "Have a super day at school, honey." A great many sacrifices are worth making to allow us to be with our children at these critical times – to support him while he's eating, to encourage her while she's getting ready for school. We can't do this by tucking notes even under the most wholesome of breakfasts.

It grieves me to think of a child finding one of these cards under the pillow at night: "I wish I were there to tuck you in." I can't help but ask how many children's problems can be traced to this simple lack of time given them by parents, grandparents, and other adults they love. The time we spend on our children when they are young will be more than repaid when they reach their teenage years.

5. Take Time for Reflection

In order to slow down, we should always take the time needed to pause and reflect. This is not only a necessary part of slowing down; it is one of the rewards too. And because it adds to efficiency and effectiveness in any walk of life, it is a very good use of time.

People today are afraid they can't afford to take time to reflect before making a responsible decision. One particularly ominous example of this development is in politics. Because news has become virtually instantaneous, everyone knows about developments and disasters around the globe as soon as they happen, and we expect people in the public eye to have immediate answers. A great many politicians now function with the motto "He who hesitates is lost." But does this really lead to responsible solutions, or just unfortunately inadequate "quick fixes"?

Of course, there *are* situations when immediate action is required, when there is no time to pause and think. But such emergencies are much rarer than we think, and the best way to prepare for them is to learn to stay calm and pause to think when circumstances are pressuring us to hurry.

This skill is applicable everywhere. At my university in India, which followed the British system, final examinations were tightly administered and observed the time limit to the minute. This naturally put students under a good deal of pressure, and almost all of them would start writing the moment the examination paper was put in their hand. But there were always a few who would pause to study the choice of essays, choose the ones they could answer best, and plan their time; only then would they begin to write. And generally they would do well – sometimes better than a brighter student who plunged in to answer without thinking.

Whether it is an exam, a report at work, or even just a reply to a letter, it always helps to stop and reflect over just what we need to say. We need to remind ourselves to take the time for reflection, for observation, for original thinking.

If we are trying to slow down the pace of our lives, we should never forget that time is precious. Time is the very stuff of which our life is made. We don't have time to waste. "As if you could kill time," Thoreau observed, "without injuring eternity."

Increasingly, the popular press itself is raising these questions, which shows how much all of us are feeling the pressures. Some years ago *Time* magazine ran a cover story entitled "Has America Run out of Time?" In it the reporters related an incident in Florida where a man billed his ophthalmologist ninety dollars for keeping him waiting an hour. "If time is valuable for my ophthalmologist," he seemed to be asking, "why isn't it valuable for me?"

I could only sympathize with him. I remember having to take a physical examination in which I was led to a little cell, told to undress, and asked to wait in a paper robe with a thermometer in my mouth for a doctor who was at least thirty minutes late. Shivering for half an hour in a paper robe is unpleasant enough to make one ask, like the man in Florida, "If their time is valuable, why isn't mine?"

6. Don't Let Yourself Get Hurried

Of course, it is terribly difficult in today's world not to be forced to hurry by circumstances. But that is precisely why it is so important.

Often, after hearing me talk about slowing down, an individual will come up and say, "What you say sounds good, but you don't know my job situation. I *have* to hurry."

Jobs do vary widely, of course. But I have been told by an emergency medical technician doing ambulance work that it *is* possible to resist being hurried even in the midst of frantic circumstances. In fact, this friend told me, that is just when he needs to keep his mind cool, concentrated, and clear. In such situations, the hands and brain of a paramedic or nurse or firefighter have been highly trained. They know what to do, and they carry out their duties swiftly. A speeded-up mind only gets in the way. (In a later chapter I will give you some effective techniques for staying slow and concentrated when people are trying to speed you up.)

Second, with some reflection, it is possible to avoid a great many situations where we know we are going to be pressured to speed up. If we look at our home life and our work, we may see that a surprising number of these situations form recurrent patterns and can be forestalled – often by the simple expedient of not waiting until the last minute to do something that needs to be done. If we cannot avoid these circumstances, it helps to be forewarned. Eventually, we may find ways of escaping a predicament in which we thought we had no choice.

Many, many pressures in our modern way of life militate against slowing down. Hurry is built into our culture; the more you look, the more instances you will see.

Once again, I got my first lesson in this in Berkeley. Shattuck Avenue is a wide, busy street, and the city authorities in those days had just added signs to the traffic signals that told when to wait and when to walk. I hadn't seen this in India and thought it was a thoughtful touch. I would wait at the corner until the sign flashed "Walk." But when I was halfway across, it would suddenly command: "Wait!" I always wanted to object, "I haven't crossed yet! If you want me to stop on this busy street, I'm not likely to make it home in one piece."

I used to see people hurry to cross that street before the light changed, dragging little children behind them. I remember one old man holding up a pleading hand as he tried to hurry, as if to beg the cars not to run over him. And that was thirty years ago. How much more hectic the pace is today! I can imagine the day when the signal will say "Wait" and then, more honestly, "Run!" And we will obey, running across the street in the unquestioned belief that it is right for us to be so hurried.

In many ways, major and minor, we are pressured by our society to go faster, faster, faster. That is why every one of us can benefit by planning our day and going through our tasks with concentration at a slow, even pace which does not put us under undue pressure. When a situation arises that does require us to speed up, we should return as quickly as possible to our usual calm, thoughtful pace.

7. Respond with Patience

Patience is one of life's unsung virtues. When people write about love, they use capital letters, italics, and calligraphy; everybody gives love the red carpet treatment. But where patience is concerned, who cares? Nobody writes poems about patience. There are no popular songs about it. If there is any reference to patience anywhere, it is in a line where it occupies an unstressed position because the word contains two syllables and fits the meter.

This is quite unfair, because patience is the very heart of love. I don't think any skill in life is more valuable. Patience is the best insurance I know against all kinds of emotional and physical problems – and it is absolutely essential for learning to slow down.

Patience may not be one of our native assets. Very few today are born with it. But everyone can learn to develop patience. As with slowing down, all we have to do to learn patience is to try to be patient every time life challenges us. And there are many, many opportunities to practice patience every day.

Work, of course, offers plenty of such opportunities.

But for most of us, the very best training ground is the home.

When my two nieces, Meera and Geetha, were ten and seven, they came to California to live with us for a few years to keep my mother company. I learned a lot about patience at their hands.

I still remember the first time we took them shopping to get their back-to-school things. It was their first year in an American school, so this was a most important trip. But I had never gone back-to-school shopping in my life. The whole concept was strange to me. When a new school year began in Kerala, we bought our books from the headmaster, and that was all.

Fortunately, Christine understood exactly what was necessary. We went from place to place with her leading the way. But at one point she and my sister had to go off to another department of the store, and I was left with the little girls to buy their remaining requirements. And once we arrived in the department they wanted, I realized that I didn't have the slightest idea of what we were looking for.

The first item was bobby pins. I had seen bobby pins, and I can recognize them in a pinch; so after a while we succeeded in finding them. But then they said they needed rubber bands, and this I couldn't follow. Rubber bands? I had seen newspapers delivered with rubber bands around them, and I had heard of people wearing headbands – in fact, when my hair once got a little long, Christine threatened to put a headband around my head to make me "look like a real Indian." But I couldn't picture little girls wearing rubber bands like that, or imagine why anyone would need them to go to school.

Finally they found the rubber bands on their own and showed me how they wore them in their hair. "Fine," I said, with only the slightest hint of impatience. "You have got your bobby pins now and your rubber bands. Is there anything more?"

"Yes," they replied. "Barrettes."

Now, I have always felt that my English vocabulary is rather large. But I had never come across this word *barrettes*. Perhaps I hadn't understood their accent. Did they mean the Barretts of Wimpole Street? Was I missing some literary allusion?

I wanted to say, "You don't need barrettes to go back to school!" And I could have added some other observations, too: about how busy I am, and how many things I have to do, and how, whatever they might be, I don't have time for barrettes.

But I knew that children are very keen observers, and I felt I had to set them an example of patience. So I said cheerfully, "All right, if it is barrettes you want, I am for it, though I don't know what they are."

They started searching, and I joined in. My nieces were impressed. Here was their uncle, who doesn't know a barrette from his beret, prepared to accompany them without even knowing what to look for.

Children, as I said, are ruthless observers. When you say that patience is a virtue, they want to know if you believe it, and they can do all sorts of things to put you to a test. If you come through that test, you have conveyed the lesson of patience.

8. Slow Down the Mind

Last, I want to say a few words about learning to slow down inside. This is the real crux of slowing down: beginning to slow down internally, in the mind.

During the early days of my teaching career, I had the privilege of meeting a Sufi whose name is well known in this country: Meher Baba. The key to his message was expressed in simple, memorable words: "A mind that is fast is sick. A mind that is slow is sound. A mind that is still is divine."

This quiet statement, so apparently out of step with the modern world, is actually both wise and extremely practical. But to understand it, even intellectually, requires some digression into the nature of the mind. To make such an abstract topic intelligible, I would like to compare the mind with something familiar: television.

I had my first exposure to television on the campus of the University of Minnesota back in 1959. I had chosen to live in the dorms, and the long months of a Minneapolis winter gave me plenty of opportunity to sit in front of the tube with the students. Usually, I confess, I wasn't watching the screen; I was watching them. Seeing their absorption gave me a clue to how much similarity there is between what happens on the screen and what happens in the mind.

Imagine that the mind is a kind of television with thoughts constantly changing channels. In this case, though, the remote control device is out of our hands; the mind is changing channels on its own. Sometimes, when a thought succeeds in holding our attention, the mind actually settles on a particular show. At other times, when we are speeded up, the mind is racing through split-second shots like a frantic rock music video.

All negative thoughts – anger, fear, passion, compulsive craving – tend to be fast. If we could see the mind when it is caught in such thoughts, we would really see it racing. But positive thoughts like love, patience, tenderness, compassion, and understanding are slow – not turbulent, rushing brooks of thinking, so to speak, but broad rivers that are calm, clear, and deep.

Anger, for example, makes the mind speed up dramatically – often "so fast you can't see straight." And that has an effect on the body. The next time you get angry, check your vital signs; you will notice your breathing in a race with your heart. When I see somebody in a fury, I get concerned, because I see it as one-thousandth of a heart attack.

With fear, the same deleterious changes take place: you breathe faster and faster, the heart beats faster and faster; all sorts of physiological processes speed up. In greed, too, whether it is greed for profit or greed for pleasure, the story is the same. And that is one way in which these negative emotional states take their toll on health.

Of course, diet and exercise play a very important part in health. I am very careful about both. But I know that even if we eat right and exercise right, if we are tormented by negative thoughts – if we are the victims of chronic anger, greed, or fear – no amount of good nutrition and aerobics will protect us against the ravages of an untrained mind.

Here I can actually say something good about television: at least even the worst addicts watch only, say, six hours per day of TV, while the internal station is on twenty-four hours a day. Our internal channel is broadcasting all the time. The mental TV is never turned off. During the day, during the night, this constant broadcasting is influencing our behavior.

Unfortunately, most people use the mind for negative thinking. Not only about others, but about themselves. In fact, a fast mind is synonymous with negative thinking – and with thinking about thinking. Just as the students I saw in Minneapolis were mesmerized by the TV, we are mesmerized by thinking. Thinking about thinking about thinking – we get entangled, and just can't come out of that labyrinth. It's like one of those big buildings on the University of California campus – Dwinelle Hall, for example – where freshmen scurry down corridor after corridor, and trot up and down the stairs, getting more and more confused, and fear that they will never be able to find their classrooms.

Many of the problems that most of us have can be solved by gaining a little detachment from our minds – to understand that some of these problems are not real. The most difficult problem to solve is the problem that is not real, at which most people work continuously.

Detachment from the mind enables us to distinguish between what is real, where we need to make a consistent effort to solve the problem, and what is unreal, where we say there is no need to solve that problem because there is no problem.

Even though we may not achieve what Meher Baba calls the still mind, the more we slow down the thinking process, the more control we have – and the less likely we are to be caught in the labyrinth of thinking about thinking.

For, as he says, a mind that is slow is sound. When your mind stops racing, it is naturally concentrated rather than distracted, naturally kind instead of rude, naturally loving instead of selfish. That is simply the dynamics of the mind. People who don't easily get provoked, even when there is cause for provocation, don't "fly off the handle." It's difficult to upset them, difficult to speed up their minds. They can stay calm in the midst of pressure, remain sensitive to the needs of all involved, see clearly, and act decisively. During a crisis – from a minor emergency at the office to a major earthquake – such people help everyone else to stay clearheaded. They are protecting not only themselves from danger, but those around them too.

CHAPTER THREE
One Thing at a Time

*E*VERY ONE OF US, I think, has times when the mind starts playing one of its old tapes – "He did this to me; she said that to me" – and just won't be switched off. Our emotions can get so stirred up that we cannot sleep, we cannot eat, we cannot let that memory go. At such times, the skill we need is the ability to turn our attention completely away from that old incident – to withdraw attention from the past and bring it back to the present.

I have talked to people caught in old resentments like this and tried to console them. "When did this quarrel take place?"

They answer glumly, "Seven years ago. In Minneapolis."

I tell them, "You are not in Minneapolis any longer; you are here in California. And it's no longer 1987; it is now 1994."

It is not an incident in the past that agitates our mind at times like these. It is the attention we give

CHAPTER THREE

the thought of that incident now. The more attention, the bigger the incident appears. Without attention, it is simply a ghost from the past.

That is why the training of attention is such an important part of bringing the mind to a calmer, more peaceful state. Along with slowing down, we need to learn how to keep our mind focused – and one of the most effective ways to learn this is to do, with complete attention, only one thing at a time.

★

Trying to get through life without control over your attention is a little like trying to reach a destination with no control over your car.

Suppose you get into your car at five o'clock as usual, ready to drive straight home after a long day at work. Unbeknown to you, however, your car has taken on a life of its own. To outward appearance it is still your reliable old Ford station wagon, but under the hood it has been possessed by a ghost.

You get in and head for home – north, say, out of San Francisco, across the Golden Gate Bridge. It is a beautiful day, and you are enjoying the view and the unusually light traffic when suddenly, without warning, your car swerves into the right-hand lane. You grab the wheel sharply, but the car ignores the wheel and pulls off onto the exit to Sausalito. In horror, you realize that you are not driving your Ford any more; it is driving you.

You want to go home, but your car has other ideas. It finds Sausalito tempting. Even a ghost is susceptible to

fine seascapes and good restaurants. You are in a panic.
What is the matter with this car?

After a desperate struggle, your Ford begins to respond to the steering wheel again, and you manage to
get back on the freeway. "Whew," you say to yourself.
"That was a strange incident. But everything seems all
right now. I just hope I can get home before anything
else happens."

Your worries are well founded. As you pass Mill
Valley, you again feel an irresistible tug on the wheel.
The ghost takes over once more, pulling fiendishly to
the right to get off the road. After fighting with you for a
few exits, it gets its way and careens off at Paradise
Drive. The malls on both sides of the highway are full of
shops your ghost finds fascinating, but you hardly notice. All you want is to get back to Highway 101.

It's a fight like this all the way home. When you
finally arrive, three or four excursions later, you're out
of gas and it's almost morning — time to head back to
San Francisco to go to work again.

This story belongs in the realm of science fiction, but
when it comes to our attention, we often have as little
control over it as the driver of this ghost-driven car.
With temptations and distractions on every side of us,
we are used to the mind weaving all over the road,
swerving from lane to lane and causing danger to ourselves and everyone around.

The next time you wash the dinner dishes, for example, see how many times your thoughts wander in just
fifteen minutes. You may watch your mind stray to the

quarrel you had with your boyfriend or girlfriend over some absurd little disagreement. It flickers back to the pan you are scrubbing, but only for a moment; then it is off again. The suds remind you of snow, and your unruly thoughts wander back to Christmases past. A few strains of "I'm Dreaming of a White Christmas" float through your mind. You are no longer standing in front of a sink in California; you are two thousand miles away in the depths of a Minnesota winter. (I experienced one of these winters at the University of Minnesota, when the temperature reached twenty below. When my American friends there sang "I'm Dreaming of a White Christmas," I replied, "I'm dreaming of a *warm* Christmas – just like the ones I used to know.")

From dishes in Petaluma to snows in Minnesota – this happens in the thinking process of everybody. We like to say we were thinking those thoughts, but it would be more accurate to say our thoughts think us.

★

Fortunately, you don't have to put up with this. Attention can be trained, and no skill in life is greater than the capacity to direct your attention at will.

The benefits of this are numerous. If you have trained your mind to give complete attention to one thing at a time, you can achieve your goal in any walk of life. Whether it is science or the arts or sports or a profession, concentration is a basic requirement in every field. And complete concentration is genius.

I have a friend who is an excellent driver with a

first-rate car. On a long-distance trip she glides smoothly into the through lane and cruises straight to her destination without even changing lanes. She never seems to exert herself, and she always manages to think a little ahead. Streams of traffic just part like the Red Sea before Moses to let her through. And her concentration is like that too. When she is behind the wheel, her mind is steady and her attention never wavers.

This kind of one-pointed attention is helpful in whatever job you are doing. But perhaps the greatest benefit of a trained mind is the emotional stability it brings. In order to get angry, your concentration must be broken – your mind has to change lanes. In order to get afraid, your mind has to change lanes. In order to get upset, your mind has to change lanes. It is not that you choose to let your attention wander; your mind simply takes over and changes whether you want it to or not. If you can keep your mind in one lane, your concentration is unbroken; you are master of your attention. Whatever the circumstances, whatever the challenges, you will not lose your sovereignty over your thinking process.

A wandering mind is not just a modern problem. Even in the days of the Compassionate Buddha, more than twenty-five hundred years ago, people used to complain to him, "I have problems at home. I have problems at work. I can't sleep well; I can't eat well; I am always upset."

The Buddha would look at them with his wise eyes and say, "Nobody is upsetting you. Nothing is upsetting you. You get upset because you are upsettable."

Then he would add, "Don't you want to be *unupset-table*?"

"Yes, Blessed One."

"Don't you want to be happy?"

"Of course, Blessed One."

"Then," he would say, "you have to train your mind."

That is what we all yearn for – a mind that cannot be upset by anything. And we can achieve it, too: but it calls for a lot of work in the training of attention.

The Buddha was perhaps the most acute psychologist the world has seen, because he understood the workings of the mind from the inside. When we have resentments or hostilities or ill will, he would say, not only our attention but our vital energy is caught in the past. When we learn to recall attention from the past and keep it completely in the present, we reclaim a tremendous reserve of vital energy that has been trapped in the past like a dinosaur. Every time we do this, we restore a little more of our vital wealth to the present moment.

Just as all of us carry the burden of resentments from the past, we all have fears and anxieties related to the future. This is part of our conditioning as human beings. But here, too, we can learn to prevent our energy from wandering into the future and keep it completely in the present.

In the long run – I am anticipating many years of training attention – you won't think about the past at all. It is not that you cannot remember the past; you just don't think about it. You won't think about the future, either: not that you don't plan for the future, but you are not entangled in what it will bring. You live one hundred percent in the present – which means you are one hundred percent alive.

★

Until it is trained, the mind will continue to go its own way, because it is the nature of an untrained mind to wander. If your mind were to appear on one of those late-night television talk shows, David Letterman would ask it, "Why do you keep wandering like this?"

And the mind would say, "I never got no education! I never got sent to school. Everybody says to me, 'It's a free world. Do what you like.'"

That is why all of us have wandering minds: it is just lack of training. But just as any great physical skill – tennis, soccer, gymnastics, skiing, skating – is acquired, through persistent practice under the guidance of an experienced coach, we can learn to train the mind.

When we are listening to a lecture or reading a book on slowing down, how is it that strange, irrelevant thoughts arise – thoughts about a restaurant that has just opened, or the new swimming pool, or what we will do if we win the lottery? After all, what we want is to listen or read with complete attention; we're not encouraging any extraneous thoughts to arise. Nonetheless, here they are: thoughts of the most unexpected kind, barging in and out without so much as a by-your-leave.

CHAPTER THREE

To some extent, I absorbed the skill of one-pointed attention early in life. My grandmother, my spiritual teacher, was constantly teaching me in many little ways – especially by her personal example – to do one thing at a time.

I will always remember sitting down one morning to my usual breakfast of iddlis (a kind of rice cake, which my granny cooked to perfection) and coconut chutney. I was so partial to this combination that on one occasion I ate twelve iddlis in a sitting. My mother was afraid I would have severe tummy trouble, so she asked in alarm, "Do you know how many you have eaten?" Before I could reply, my granny said, "This is not a café. Let him eat. It won't do him any harm." That is how fond I was of rice cakes and coconut chutney.

On this particular morning, however, I had got absorbed in a book by Washington Irving. I had just discovered the delightful story of Rip Van Winkle, a fellow who could sleep for twenty years. I was holding the book with my left hand and reading, while my right hand was taking a rice cake, dipping it in the chutney, and putting it into my mouth.

Even then, my capacity for concentration was rather good. And, as I told you, I loved a good book. So I must have been immersed in the adventures of Rip Van Winkle for some time before I noticed that there was nothing in my right hand and nothing was going into my mouth. I turned to look and saw that the plate was gone, the iddlis were gone, the chutney was gone. I had just been moving an empty hand to my mouth.

I was indignant. "Who took my iddlis away?" I demanded. "You weren't even tasting the iddlis," my granny said. "You were reading. You didn't even know I took them away. That is poor reading and poor eating." She wouldn't give me my breakfast until I had put the book away.

Doing something else while we eat is such a common habit today that no one even questions it. If you go to any restaurant in the business district at lunchtime, you will see any number of hurried executives lunching off the *Wall Street Journal*. You can watch as one morsel of salad is consumed and then one morsel of *Journal*. That is poor eating and poor business practice, too. If I were to select a stockbroker, which is rather unlikely, I would try to find one who knows how to keep his concentration on salad when he is eating and on the *Wall Street Journal* when he is planning my investments.

Much more alarming, I see people talking on their cellular phones while they drive. They say, "You can call me anytime, anywhere." As if this were an advantage! Imagine, they never have a moment when they can be sure they won't be interrupted – not while they are driving, not even while they are walking down the street. In fact, such inventions as cellular phones and computers actually encourage our tendency to do two or more things at once.

For students, the practice of one-pointed attention is essential. Complete concentration is necessary for learning. But go to any great university and see how many are doing two or more things at a time – listening to music, drinking coffee, smoking, talking, and then trying to study at the same time. When the time comes for a grade, they are likely to get "Incomplete" – not a grade we had in India, but one that seems quite appropriate for divided attention.

You will find that if you have a concentrated mind, you won't need as many hours to study. You will remember vividly what you have read and heard. It saves a lot of time, and it will give you valuable self-assurance for writing your papers and finals.

★

One-pointed attention is most rewarding in personal relationships, where nothing can be more important than giving complete attention to one another. This is particularly true with children. Children naturally ask all kinds of questions and take a long time to tell their stories, and in millions of homes the parents are reading the paper as they reply, "Yes, yes, I see." And in millions of homes, the parents are surprised when their children don't listen to them.

Those little bright eyes know when your attention is wandering. When they are telling you the news from school, give your full attention. Everything else can be set aside for the moment. You are training your children to listen to you.

That is how I was trained by my grandmother and my mother. Every day, when I came back from school, my grandmother would say, "Tell me everything from the time you left home until the time you came back."

All my news was important to her. She gave me her un-divided attention as I went through the events of the day from English class through the soccer game and the swim in the river after school. Children need this, and we need time for listening to their stories, which they tell at their own pace. Giving them things is not a substi-tute for our time and our undivided attention.

In Zen, they say when you are listening to the roshi, the Zen master, your eyes should not wander even for a moment. I think that is good advice for any occasion. When somebody is talking to you, give your full atten-tion. Eyes, ears, mind, and heart should be focused on the person you are listening to. He or she can't help re-sponding to your wholehearted attention. Every con-versation is an opportunity for training the mind to be one-pointed.

Today, after years of training, complete concentra-tion comes naturally to me. Even if what the other per-son is saying is not of urgent interest to me, I find it natural to concentrate. My mind doesn't wander, and neither do my eyes.

I can't help but notice how common the opposite is. Watch people at a social gathering. How many are really giving their full attention to the person they are talking with? There may be a lot of animated conversa-tion and an air of conviviality in the room, but if you ob-serve carefully, you will see that most people's eyes are wandering. It means their minds are wandering too.

Once, after attending a warm social occasion at the home of a friend, I asked my hostess, "Why do people have these short, scattered conversations? It seemed to me that no one was really paying attention to anyone else."

"Most people are 'working the room,'" she replied candidly. "They want to be sure to say at least a few words to everyone who is there, and it really doesn't matter what the words are so long as they are pleasant and reach all the important people. So you're always looking around to see who has just come in.

"Besides," she added, "no one wants to get caught in a boring conversation. So everybody keeps looking around to see if there is someone more interesting to talk with."

I couldn't help thinking that if you can't keep your attention in one place, how can anything *not* be boring? Nothing can be interesting, after all, unless you give it your attention.

Effortless concentration is the secret of all personal relationships, whether it is with casual acquaintances, co-workers, colleagues, friends, or family. And when relationships are not particularly cordial, one-pointed attention is even more important. It is an exceptional person who can give complete attention to somebody who is being unpleasant. When you can do this, you can slowly disarm even a hostile person simply by listening without hostility, with complete and even loving attention. In my own long experience, no thrill is greater than that of winning over a tough opponent to be an ally.

In life we are going to come across opposition everywhere, especially when we are doing original, worthwhile work. Instead of becoming resentful or afraid, we can learn to look upon every opponent as a possible supporter and every piece of criticism as a way to grow. These are the challenges we need in order to learn how to win over opposition, to turn a difficult situation into an opportunity, and to transform our own negative qualities into strengths.

I vividly remember watching one of the best matches I have ever seen in tennis: John McEnroe against Mats Wilander. It was a sustained fight in which every play was countered by one of equal skill. I kept telling my friends, "I don't care who wins. It is of no consequence to me who gets the cup and who doesn't. What I enjoy is seeing these great players equally challenged, because it brings out the best in each of them." That is how I see life: not somebody winning and somebody else losing, but each of us growing as difficulties and challenges draw us up to our best.

When you see opposition, therefore, do not get afraid. If you can keep your concentration unbroken, you can look on tough opposition as a challenge to test your capacities, so that through patience, courtesy, and the depth of your conviction, you can win over even the fiercest opponent.

But all this takes time to develop. You have to be willing to work at developing these skills. Many people today admire the ability to stay firm, calm, and compassionate under attack; but they are not prepared to develop the capacity – in part because it doesn't come immediately, and because their attention is distracted by other goals.

★

Everywhere, you can learn to focus your attention by doing one thing at a time.

There used to be an eating place in Berkeley called Chat and Chew. I never wanted to eat there. When I am chewing, I want to chew; when I am chatting, I want to chat. If I am enjoying a plate of fettucini, I don't want to discuss the weather, watch television, listen to music, or read the paper; I want to enjoy my meal. Even when I am having a cup of decaf, I prefer to enjoy my drink first and then give full attention to the conversation.

The Buddha said, "When you are walking, walk. When you are sitting, sit. Don't wobble." I paraphrase him in modern American idiom: "When you are drinking decaf, drink decaf. When you are chatting, chat. Don't wobble." We need this advice today because we spend most of our time wobbling. We find it all but impossible to do just one thing at a time.

Years ago I went to see *Romeo and Juliet* presented by the Royal Shakespeare Company in San Francisco. It was a great occasion for me, because I had taught the play countless times – in fact, I had been introduced to it when I was about Romeo's age myself, in my little village school. I knew every important passage by heart and was deeply moved by the Royal Shakespeare presentation.

During the second act, I was thrilling to that paean to

youthful love in which Romeo cries, "It is the east, and Juliet is the sun," when I heard a soft female voice rather unlike Juliet's implore, "Where is the candy, please?"

I didn't remember teaching that line in Shakespeare.

Then, with more urgency, the voice came again: "Where is the candy?"

I looked around and saw two high school girls who were sharing a box of candy. My grandmother, who could be blunt, would have told them, "You don't know how to enjoy a play, and you don't know how to enjoy candy either."

When we do things with only a part of the mind, we are just skimming the surface of life. Nothing sinks in; nothing has real impact. It leads to an empty feeling inside. Unfortunately, it is this very emptiness that drives us to pack in even more, seeking desperately to fill the void in our hearts. What we need to do is just the opposite: to slow down and live completely in the present. Then every moment will be full.

A one-pointed mind makes beauty more beautiful. Music becomes more beautiful; painting becomes more beautiful; colors are more vivid and tones more dulcet. There is an inspired passage in Western mysticism where Thomas Traherne tells us that in his eyes the streets appeared to be paved with gold, and the boys and girls playing there looked like angels. "All appeared new," he says, "and strange at first, inexpressibly rare and delightful and beautiful." That is the intensification of vision, the seeing into the heart of life, which one-pointed attention brings.

★

A one-pointed mind can be cultivated throughout the day by giving your complete attention to whatever you are doing. Keep your attention undivided as far as possible.

While driving, for example, don't talk to the other people in the car. In my early days in this country, I was once a passenger in a car with a driver who had probably never heard about undivided attention. We were speeding down the highway when he launched into a heated discussion, taking issue vigorously with something I had said the day before. Naturally, I wanted to explain to him why I thought he had misunderstood. But when he took both hands off the steering wheel to emphasize his point, I immediately exclaimed, "Never mind. Whatever you say. Just keep your hands on the wheel!" I still think it saved our lives.

On another occasion, when I went to Arizona to give a talk on meditation, I was enjoying the long drive through the desert when my eyes caught sight of a sign high up on a rock. It said, "You're supposed to be watching the road." Very helpful. While driving, our hands should be on the wheel and our eyes on the road – and so should our attention.

Most of us can understand the wisdom of this when it comes to driving, but it applies in life's less dangerous situations, too. In fact, it applies to the simplest of the routine activities that make up your day. In the kitchen, for example, when you are cutting vegetables, cut vegetables. Don't talk, and don't look here and there. If somebody tries to get your attention, stop cutting and give her your full attention – or ask her politely to let you finish first. You can avoid many kitchen accidents by this simple practice, but more than that, you are teaching your mind to make one-pointed attention a habit in everything you do.

Whatever job you are engaged in – as a dentist, as a lawyer, as a carpenter or an engineer or a salesperson – concentrate completely on the task at hand. Don't be distracted by the question of how pleasant or unpleasant the job is, or how much profit or prestige it promises. As long as it is not at another person's expense, as long as it is not detrimental to people's health and well-being, give it your best. Concentrate on it completely, and do not let yourself get distracted by brooding over the results of your efforts. It will lift a great burden from your shoulders, and you will find yourself doing much better work while enjoying it more.

Similarly, when the day is done, leave your work at the office. Do not bring it home, as many people have a habit of doing. Eight hours doesn't seem to be enough for them, so after the workday is over they like to put a leash on their job and bring it home with them like a pet poodle, barking all the way.

In my experience, campus people are particularly susceptible to this. They are unable to leave their research and their papers and books and statistics on campus; they have to bring it all home with them, yapping at their heels. If you complain, they tell you, "Oh, this is not an ordinary dog. It's my pet poodle. I have to take it wherever I go." Stop them anywhere and they will tell you how their research is going or about the article they are writing. If you run into a classics scholar at the supermarket and ask politely, "How are you today?" she will reply, "Oh, I have just been comparing the metric patterns of Virgil and Homer." If you don't run away fast enough, you will get a dissertation on Latin and Greek prosody right there next to the cheese counter.

This is what I mean by bringing the poodle home: it's not just in your briefcase, but in your cranium too. It takes a lot of control to work with complete concentration for eight hours and then drop your work at will, but this is one of the greatest skills that one-pointed attention can bring. When you enter your office, you give all your attention to your job; once you leave, you put the job out of your mind. This simple skill guards against tension and allows you to give your very best. To glean from Meher Baba's insight again, if you have given your very best, there is no need to worry – and when you don't worry, you are happy.

★

The amazing development of this habit of worrying is a significant comment on our times. People put a great deal of effort into developing this habit. They practice it constantly. When they leave home, they worry about whether they have locked the door; they have got to go back and turn the key in the lock to make doubly sure. Then they realize they have left the key in the lock, and have to go back a second time to collect it. They mail a letter and then worry about whether they remembered to write the address. If we lock the door and mail our letters with our attention on what we are doing, these little problems don't arise at all.

In fact, it is in these small matters of daily life that lack of concentration shows up easily. People forget things because they do not concentrate. They worry because they don't concentrate. Here the Buddha uses a word I like very much: mindfulness. Whatever you are doing, he says, do it mindfully. Give it your full attention. We can guard ourselves against all kinds of tension by learning to be mindful in everything we do.

The person who has control over his attention will always be mindful of what he is thinking, saying, and doing. Most of us, the Buddha implies, are not aware of these things at all. He compares our ordinary state of awareness to a dream: we are thinking, talking, and living in our sleep. It is a compassionate way of describing the kind of fragmented lives we lead. It is because we are not really aware, the Buddha says, that we say and do unkind things. When we are fully here in the present, we won't say or do anything that is unkind.

★

When concentration is deep, we may forget our body completely. In fact, we may forget altogether about that dreariest of subjects, ourselves. This is the real secret of happiness.

You may have noticed that when a lover of music is

listening to a Beethoven sonata, you can tap her on the shoulder and she won't notice. All her awareness is on the music. Patanjali, an insightful teacher of meditation in ancient India, explains that this is the real reason for her enjoyment. Every ray of her attention is on the music, so there is no attention left for herself and her problems at all.

Albert Einstein had such a native genius for concentration that he often forgot completely the distinction between himself and others, between "you" and "me." One of the most delightful examples of this is a story about Einstein at a dinner party with intimate friends in Princeton. The after-dinner discussion went on and on into the small hours of the morning, until finally Einstein got up and said apologetically, "I hate to do this, but I must put you out now because I have got to be on campus tomorrow morning." "Albert," his host said, "you are in my house."

Einstein often became so absorbed in his work that he was not aware of the physical needs that dominate most people's attention. There are many stories about him that illustrate this, some of which must be apocryphal but which are illuminating nonetheless. Once, it is said, a colleague met Einstein on the street and asked him if he had had his lunch. "Tell me which way I am going," Einstein replied. "If I am going home, I haven't eaten. If I am going toward campus, I have."

This kind of absorption has its everyday difficulties, but it offers an extraordinary blessing. At a very deep level, people like this understand that the sense that you and I are separate, isolated creatures is no more than an illusion. Einstein called it "a kind of optical delusion of consciousness." To a great extent, he had lost any sense of being separate from the rest of creation. This awareness of unity is the distinguishing mark of spiritual awareness. Such people will consider you as part of themselves, and their interests as part of your own. They will consider their "me" as part of "you." They will never think to harm you, because they are part of you; they will always think kindly of you, because you are part of them.

★

You can identify people with one-pointed attention because they will be loyal in all their relationships. Those whose attention wanders easily are not capable of lasting loyalties. This is one of the pervasive problems in society today, and the answer can be rather simple: to train our attention not to wander. When our thoughts start to stray to fresh fields and pastures new, we can call them back to stay in their own field, which makes that field fresh and new every day.

The benefit of this simple skill is that when there are difficulties and differences in an intimate relationship, your loyalty will not waver. Your love will not wobble at all.

There is so much friction and conflict in personal relationships today that disloyalty may seem inevitable. I have often been asked by a man and a woman who were drifting apart, "Have we lost our capacity to love? Is it not possible for us to be loyal?" I don't reply to this as a moral issue; I present it as an engineering issue. Without the precious ability to keep your attention in the channel you choose, it is not possible to be deeply in love or consistently loyal in your relationships. It is because our contemporary culture offers no way of training attention that we find good people, sensitive people, drifting apart. I have been able to help because I don't say, "You are wrong; she is right. You are disloyal; she is loyal." I say, "You can train your attention. You can teach it how not to wander." The mind can be trained to such an extent that even if somebody you love lets you down, you can treat that person with respect and rebuild the relationship so that it is even more loving and secure.

★

Life today is full of difficulties and conflicts. I think it was Trotsky who said that anyone who wants to lead a peaceful life has chosen the wrong century in which to be born. These are tempestuous times, fraught with turmoil and violence – which means there is all the more reason to have a well-trained mind.

When you have a mind that obeys you, you don't have to run away when trouble threatens – and neither do you have to retaliate. You can receive opponents with respect and oppose them resolutely, returning good will for ill will and love for hatred. Very often, in my experience, this approach will sober an opponent enough that he responds to you with respect as well.

You train your mind to do this by switching your attention just as you change the channel on your TV set. There are many injurious channels in the mind, negative channels like anger, greed, arrogance, fear, and malice. But for every negative emotion there is a positive emotion, and you can learn to change channels.

I was at a friend's home when I learned to use a remote control to regulate the channels on his TV.

My host said, "You just point this thing at the television and change it to whatever you like."

I didn't want to see *Conan the Barbarian* or *The Terminator*, so I didn't have to put up with them. With the touch of a button, I could switch to *Pride and Prejudice* or *The Tempest* instead.

Because you have been brought up in a scientific, technological culture – not always an advantage! – you see nothing miraculous about this. There may be no visible connection between the TV and the remote control, but it works, and you take for granted that there is a scientific explanation. But I had to ask a friend who knows about electronics to explain to me how the remote control device sends a signal that allows me to change channels.

That is exactly what I do with my mind. When somebody is rude to me – which is seldom – don't think I am not aware of it. I am very much aware, but I can change the channel in my mind from anger to compassion as easily as changing channels on the TV.

Sometimes, when people see that I do not return rudeness for rudeness, they say, "He's an angel!"

I want to reply, "No angel. I just know how to direct my attention." If necessary, when someone is trying to take advantage of me, I can – in Zen language – give that person a piece of my 'no-mind' too. I know how to do that, if it's really necessary. It is not good to let people walk all over us, and occasionally we need to resist when they try. But we can resist without losing compassion and respect if we know how to keep our mind steady.

When your attention has been trained, if somebody does you a bad turn – which is very common in the world – you don't blow it up into something big. That is what attention does. When you give little discourtesies your attention, they get blown up into big balloons of frightening proportions. If you don't give them attention, you simply brush them aside.

Similarly, little cravings that should not present much of a problem – an urge to eat this, smoke that, do this, say that – get blown up to gigantic crises. We feel we have to act on them or burst. These selfish urges are part of the human condition, but often all we have to do when they come is to turn our attention away. If we can do this, we can puncture even a big temptation and watch it shrink smaller and smaller and smaller while we get bigger and bigger and bigger. It's a strange, Alice-in-Wonderland world: where we saw a temptation towering over us and threatening to devour us, we find ourselves standing tall as a giant while a tiny temptation says, "Excuse me, may I leave now?"

★

Attention can be trained very naturally, with affection, just as you train a puppy. When something distracts your attention, you say "Come back" and bring it back again. With a lot of training, you can teach your mind to come running back to you when you call, just like a friendly pup.

I am quite fond of dogs, and dogs are fond of me. When I walk on the beach, I see dogs listening to their masters or mistresses easily and joyfully. Whether it is a Great Dane or a little dachshund, the good-natured dog runs back obediently at the call of its human companion.

On one dreary occasion, however, I saw a man yelling at his dog as a drill sergeant would yell at a new recruit, and he expected the dog to salute, too. The dog did not listen to anything the man said. The man kept yelling, "Come *back!*" But the dog just came running to me.

All of the man's anger and yelling did nothing to control that dog, who just wanted to have a good run on the beach. Similarly, I would say, don't try to be drastic with the mind. Don't act like a tyrant. Just keep patiently bringing attention back to the task at hand.

Friends of mine had a dog named Muka, of whom I was very fond. Muka was a playful creature with boundless energy, and whenever he saw something running, whether it was a rabbit or a truck, he had to run after it. But he was so devoted to me that whenever I called him, even if he had taken off down the road, he would come running back.

Our attention can be like that. When it sees a memory, it has to chase it, yapping, yapping, yapping at its heels. If it catches that memory, the memory has caught us. The moment attention takes off is the time to call, "Come back!" After years of calling it back, the great day will arrive when our attention will stay where we want it without our even needing to call. This is a glorious achievement, for it means there can be no resentment, no hostility, no guilt, no anxiety, no fear. Our attention will not dwell on any wisp from the past or the future. It will rest entirely here and now.

When our attention does not retreat to the past or wander into the future, we are delivered from time into the eternal now. To rest completely in the present like this is infinite security and infinite joy. In the Upanishads, the perennial fountain of spiritual wisdom in India, the sages compute the joy of a person who has every material satisfaction the world can offer and say, "Let that be one measure of joy. One million times that is the joy of the person who rests completely on the present, for every moment is full of joy."

CHAPTER FOUR
Finding Balance

NOT LONG AGO I went with friends to a favorite restaurant overlooking San Francisco Bay. We arrived early for lunch, so even though the place is very popular, we got a good table near the window. Soon I was completely absorbed in the scene. Outside the sun was bright and the wind was high. Hundreds of seagulls were tossing about in the sky, and as many sailboats on the waves.

I don't know much about sailing, but I couldn't help admiring the skill of some of the sailors. While we watched, one boat was racing towards us over the water with its sail almost dipping into the sea. My heart leapt into my mouth, and I wanted to cry, "They're gone!" But the agile crew kept leaning out over the water on the opposite side, and the boat never quite turned over.

Others on the water were not so skillful. They would catch a strong wind in their sails and pick up impressive speed, but I would see their boats

CHAPTER FOUR

suddenly career erratically as if they had a life of their own. I could sympathize. How like life in today's restless, unpredictable world, where we often feel we are running before the wind in a stormy sea.

Below the restaurant window, scores of other boats were tied up, hugging the shore, their lines slapping idly in the breeze. On their decks, men and women in summer clothes were enjoying drinks, chatting, or reclining in lounge chairs in the sun, perhaps dreaming that they, too, were sailors – all the while their boats tied up comfortably at the dock. Most of us have days like this too: times when we just can't get going, just don't feel like moving.

But as I watched in admiration, a few brave boats were sailing sharply into the wind toward the mouth of the Golden Gate. Watching those frail vessels venturing out into the dangerous waters of the Pacific Ocean recalled to my mind the haunting words of the Compassionate Buddha: "Who wants to cross the sea of life? Is there anyone for the other shore?"

For me, the Buddha has always been an inspiring teacher because he had the skill and the sheer daring to sail boldly into the rough seas of life and reach his goal on the opposite shore. Remembering his words, I was no longer seated in a restaurant in San Francisco with my friends. I was standing at the shore listening to his call, so urgent, so personal: "Jump into your boat! Don't spend your life sleeping on the Marina and walking on the beach with the pigeons. Don't you want to sail skillfully on this turbulent sea?"

★

Most of us have seasons like these three kinds of sailors. At times we surge with energy, so much so that our lives are almost out of control. At other times we face blocks, can't seem to get on top of things, can't seem to move. Often these phases are accompanied by mood swings between high and low, ebbs and flows of self-esteem. And, of course, there are times when we maneuver gracefully through events which at other times would have hopelessly becalmed or capsized us, navigating unerringly towards our goal. That is life.

According to yoga philosophy, the human personality is a constant interplay of these three elements – inertia, energy, and harmony. All three are always present, but one tends to be dominant at any given time – in a day, throughout a stage of life, over a life itself. And they lie on a continuum of energy. Just as matter can exist as a solid, a liquid, or a gas – ice, water, or steam – our own energy-states move in and out of inertia, activity, and harmony.

Inertia, of course, is least desirable. Energetic activity is much more desirable, but without control it only consumes our time and gets us into trouble. Harmony is the state we desire to live in. Fortunately, because all three are states of the same energy, each of these states can be changed into another. Just as ice can be thawed into water and water turned into steam, inertia and activity are both full of energy which can be converted into a state of dynamic balance full of vitality and power. That is what I meant when I compared Gandhi with a skilled driver behind the wheel of a Ferrari.

★

It is wonderful to have abundant energy, for then no obstacle is too big to overcome. But there can be danger when a person has more energy than he or she knows what to do with. If we lack direction and an overriding goal, we are likely to misunderstand the signals that life sends us. Life is saying, "Come on! Venture out on the high seas, brave the adventures I send, and perfect the skills you need to fulfill your destiny." But we don't hear this message clearly. Somehow the signal gets garbled, and we can't tell where the call is coming from. So we pour our energy out into restless seeking, chasing fulfillment on Montgomery Street, with the bulls and bears at the stock exchange; or Union Street, with its fashionable boutiques; or Ghirardelli Square, where there seems to be a place to eat for every day of the year; or the night spots of North Beach. We can spend a lifetime like this and get nowhere.

Further, when we have a lot of energy we feel we have to act. We just cannot be idle. We get involved in activities and relationships primarily out of restlessness, and, because we cannot restrain ourselves even when we see the warning signs, we get into a lot of trouble.

Most of us know people like this. They have to keep going from morning till night, even doing things that are trivial. They have to keep busy, even if it means doing things that help no one including themselves. They simply cannot sit still.

One drizzly afternoon in Berkeley I was surprised to see our neighbor watering his lawn. "You know," I said in a friendly manner, "I really think it's raining. Why are you watering the lawn?" "Well, you know me," he replied. "I don't like to sit around."

I think it is Thoreau who said, "It is not enough if you are busy. The question is, What are you busy about?" This is a useful question. To know when to plunge into an activity and when to refrain from it requires judgment – detachment and discrimination. In India we have a saying, "Lack of discrimination is the greatest danger." When we lack discrimination, we do not know when to throw ourselves into something and when not to get entangled in it – and the more energy we have, the more it is going to get us involved in sticky, even dangerous situations from which it is difficult and painful to escape.

Bergson said that the human species should not be called *homo sapiens,* "the creature that thinks," but *homo faber,* "the creature that makes things." I think this is an astute observation. Most of us are concerned with making things: houses, roads, helicopters, guitars, pasta, anything. As long as we can make something, we find some satisfaction in living.

Take a walk in any large shopping mall and look in the shop windows. How many places are selling something that is necessary? How many are selling items that are beneficial? We can accommodate a whole mall in two or three shops if we rule out things which have been made just because homo faber fever has got us.

★

Energy out of control has two salient characteristics: hurry and worry.

In Berkeley I used to see dusty Volkswagen buses with their windows covered with stickers: "Paraguay," "Turista," "Mexico." We can tell the owners are travelers from the stickers they have collected – unless they just bought them in some little place on Telegraph Avenue. Similarly, if we observe a man or woman who is the victim of over-abundant energy, we will see two small identifying stickers: "Hurry" and "Worry."

Worry goes with hurry because the person in a hurry doesn't have time to think clearly and make clear decisions, so he or she is always worried about results. Drawing upon my observations of people on academic campuses, I would say that people in a hurry are likely never to be sure about the results of their work. They worry about the conclusions of their research, about the value of their work, about whether they are contributing to the welfare of their students. If you slow down enough to think clearly and act wisely, you have no need to worry because you know you are doing your best.

★

One fascinating thing about people with a lot of energy is that it's not at their beck and call. When energy is overflowing, it tends to drive them; but at other times it just dries up. This is the other pole of our lives: the times when we just can't get going.

Often people have energy only when it comes to doing things they like. We all know people who have boundless motivation when it comes to doing what they want to do. They get absorbed in details that seem excruciating to us and pass hours without noticing how much time has gone by. But when it comes to activities that don't interest them, they may actually seem sluggish and even lacking in energy.

Most of us are like this. We have energy for activities that interest us, but when that energy is blocked it flows elsewhere, to something more attractive. We get busy doing those other, more attractive things and can't find time for what needs doing.

In India we call this "painting the bullock cart wheels." Just when the harvest is ready to be brought in, the farmer notices that the wheels of his bullock cart are looking rather shabby. Instead of going out into the fields, he takes a day to go into town for paint and then spends a week painting beautiful designs on the cart wheels. When he finally gets around to harvesting the rice, he has to work twelve hours a day just to keep up.

Even people who are usually energetic can have

a mental block when a challenge comes to them. Students often grind to a halt on the eve of finals and find it physically impossible to open a book. I have seen students in Berkeley dismantling their motorcycles the night before exams, which calls for a lot more energy and application than the study of Wordsworth's "Ode to Immortality." This is a valuable clue: the problem is not lack of energy, but how to control and direct it.

Adults, of course, don't usually have to write papers on Wordsworth. But we do have to fill out our tax returns each year, turn in reports at work, write thank-you notes, clean out garages, and perform countless other tasks that most of us find distasteful. How many of us decide to put such things off while we work on our car or plant the new vegetable garden instead? Cars and gardens do need attention, but tax returns are urgent. In fact, when the calendar says April 14th, anything else is a distraction.

The energetic, restless, aggressive person is often looked upon as an achiever – a valuable asset who accomplishes much. People who are driven by their own energy can be like steamrollers, rolling relentlessly over any obstacle in their way. Yet when they face a task which promises no personal profit or power, the steamroller may become a rolling stone, perhaps even a sitting stone. Then it cannot push away obstacles; it can only roll, if that.

★

Physically, inertia is a feeling that you just can't move; mentally, it is a sluggish mind. Even if you try to be sensitive, if your mind is sluggish, you just don't feel anything intensely. You may even see a tragedy enacted in front of your eyes and not be able to respond meaningfully. You may see one person exploiting another, one group persecuting another, and not be able to get angry. Your energy is frozen. You are not deliberately refusing to act; you just don't have the capacity.

Having a lot of energy has advantages as well as disadvantages, but inertia has no advantages at all. It is much, much better to have energy and get into trouble than not to be able to move. One of the most tragic phrases in English is "I don't care." When we are caught in inertia, we are saying, "I don't care what happens to anybody, including myself."

But inertia is frozen power. The power *is* there. Just as water can freeze, thaw, and freeze again, our personal energy surges back and forth between activity and torpor.

Look at what happens with most of us when we start a fitness program. We see some show on TV over the weekend and are filled with enthusiasm; we get expensive shoes and a fashionable outfit and go to bed Sunday night with the alarm set to go off early for a half-hour run before a good, nutritious breakfast. And for a week the schedule works perfectly. We have a keen appetite after the run, enjoy a nourishing breakfast, and feel invigorated for the rest of the day – all week long.

But when Saturday morning dawns and the alarm goes off, we're tired and sore. And after all, it *is* Saturday. There's no clock to punch at work. What does it matter if we have our run a little later? It's rather boring, and anyhow, rest is important too.

By the time we wake up without the alarm, the sun is high and we remember we have a number of other things we need to do. There really isn't much time for a run. Still, it's part of the program, so we drag ourselves out of bed and lumber out onto the pavement. But activity seems less invigorating when the chill is off the air, and we feel self-conscious now that people are on the street. After fifteen minutes we hit the wall and decide to call it enough.

It's almost eleven when we get to breakfast. Since it's Saturday, we follow the nutritious part of the meal with a sweet roll, and wash it down with three cups of strong coffee to get going.

By afternoon, serious difficulties have set in. Someone has lent us an old paperback on UFOs and aliens, and it's just been lying around. It doesn't look particularly elevating, but we really should glance at it before we give it back. Remarkably, it proves rather gripping. After a few pages, we settle down on the couch and get into a comfortable reading position on our back. There is a package of cookies on the table, and we take one or two while we read. One or two won't hurt.

Eventually we realize that our hand is scraping th

bottom of the bag. In fact, only one cookie remains.
We're not particularly hungry any more, but we might
as well eat it. We go on reading, and soon we have fallen
asleep. We wake up just in time for dinner.

All in all, not such a good day for our fitness program. But it is better than the following day, Sunday,
when we can't seem to rouse ourselves out of bed at all.

We have a phrase for this in India: "a hero at the beginning." Plenty of energy at the start, but it fizzles out.

Or the energy cycle may start at the other pole. Years
ago I saw an entertaining film about one of those rather
seedy detectives whom you grow to love. I have forgotten most of the film, but the opening scene is still vivid.
When the fellow drags himself out of bed in the morning he has a three-day growth of beard and can't even
open his eyes. His movements are so sluggish that you
think he must have been worked over by gangsters or
be suffering from a serious hangover, but it turns out
he's just a slow starter. He manages to get to the kitchen
for a strong cup of coffee, and then discovers that he ran
out a day or two before. Fortunately he hasn't washed
the percolator in a while. He finds it in the pile of other
unwashed dishes, pours boiling water over the grounds,
and drinks the result with a grimace while he lights a
cigarette. We want to ask, "This is the hero? He can't
even get himself dressed!" But then the phone rings, and
the transformation begins. There's a crisis, someone's
been killed, and within minutes this slow starter is a
man of action.

Fortunately, there is a state beyond both phases of

this cycle – beyond restless activity and sluggish inactivity too. The energy frozen as inertia can be released, and then all our energy brought under control in a dynamic balance that allows us to give our best and enjoy life to the fullest.

First, when we are frozen, we can thaw out. None of us need be stuck in inertia. Enthusiasm and energy are qualities that all of us come into life with – just look at an infant! – and although some people have them in more abundance, everyone can cultivate them. I know how difficult it is to thaw the cold block of indifference, but it can be done through the systematic practice of meditation and the related methods of the Eight-Point Program.

I appreciate the person who is energetic by nature, but I have special admiration when I see someone who suffers from lethargy learn to turn it into a torrent of activity. Vigor, vitality, energy, and will can all be developed. I have seen really lackadaisical men and women turn into dynamos through this program. When they visit home again or go to a high school reunion, people say, "I don't believe it's you! You used to get up at ten and take an hour to eat breakfast. I've never seen you work so hard. What happened to you?"

Everyone likes a man or woman who has gusto and enthusiasm, but it is not enough to have an enthusiastic attitude and lapse when it comes to action. We need the energy and will to carry out our good intentions in whatever field of action we choose. Otherwise, even if we are enthusiastic, we won't be able to follow through; inertia will block our way. If we take to painting, we won't get beyond buying paints and canvas; if we decide to learn a language, we will get the books and tapes but not find time for Lesson 2.

★

Inertia is like driving with your brakes on. A surprising number of people do this; their brakes are set all the time.

When I was learning to drive, Christine offered to instruct me, though I think she felt rather insecure when I was behind the wheel. In those days traffic in Berkeley was usually light, so after I reached a certain level of proficiency she told me I could practice on the streets when it was not the rush hour.

Once, when we were going along Bancroft next to the university – where, fortunately, the speed limit was twenty-five miles per hour – we began to smell something like burning rubber. Christine was distressed, but the car seemed to be functioning all right and we were almost home, so I continued to drive – rather slowly, which suited me – until we reached our house on Walnut Street. It was only then that we discovered the emergency brake had been on the whole time. I didn't know it was even possible to drive that way. Now I know, so if I ever smell that smell again I will ask the driver, "Say, are your brakes on?"

That is just what happens when we are in a state of

inertia. We may have gas in the tank and an engine in top condition, but no amount of potential power helps if we drive when the brakes are on. On the other hand, it means there is no irremediable problem. All that is required is to release the brake.

When energy surges, we have the opposite problem: no brakes at all. Then we can't stop. We have to move, have to act, have to get involved – which means we can get caught in virtually any activity under the sun.

Sometimes what begins as a hobby becomes a life-long occupation – or obsession. I have seen this happen many, many times on academic campuses. Someone takes up the study of punctuation in order to correct student papers and discovers there are several schools of thought about how to use the comma. He begins to tell colleagues about it. After a while he is giving lectures about where the comma should be used and where it should be a colon or semicolon. Before he knows it, the fate of the world depends on whether it should be a comma or a colon.

Often – though not always! – what we get caught in is something we think we like. But after a while we can't think about anything else. I have known many people who tell me that they think about their work day and night because they really enjoy what they do. But they can't turn it off. They can't keep from taking their work home or staying late at the office instead of seeing their family, and they can't turn off their minds when it's time to sleep. While you are talking to them, they are not really listening to you but thinking about their work or their hobby. They may not realize it, but what once seemed so pleasant to think about has become a burden.

"I'm a fashion designer," a woman once told me after a talk. "I love what I do. I'm always designing, even when I'm with my children. I get some of my best ideas that way."

"I understand," I told her. "I loved teaching literature so much that I felt embarrassed to be paid for doing something I so enjoyed. But today I can't say I'm enjoying anything unless it's done in freedom."

We can get caught in anything: in fashion, in collecting things, in shopping, in furniture, in yard sales. We can easily get caught in cars and food. We can even get caught in houseplants; that's why every shopping mall has a little "plant paradise." These are the things that drain our energy and our time. And once we get caught, we begin to get speeded up, trying to keep up with where our hobby leads us. One friend confided in me that he had got caught like this in taping old movies on TV. After a while he was spending hours at it, sitting through late shows so he could avoid taping the commercials. He realized things were out of hand only when he caught himself staying up until two in the morning to tape a movie he didn't want so that he could trade it to someone in his video club. And don't you know people who complain that they have so many plants that they haven't time for anything but watering and cutting and spraying?

Now, I'm not at all saying there is anything wrong

with houseplants. But there are times to cultivate the garden inside: time to reflect on what we are doing, what we value, how we are spending our lives. *Homo faber*, "the maker," has to stop incessantly making and doing in order to become *homo sapiens* – truly wise.

We need time for pondering life's deeper questions instead of always making money or making things. We need time simply to be quiet now and then. There is an inner stillness which is healing, which makes us more sensitive and gives us an opportunity to see life whole.

★

To live in balance, we need to drive the way skilled highway patrol officers do, with one foot on the gas and the other poised over the brake. When we want power, all we need to do is press the gas pedal. And if we start to get out of control, we just tap the brake.

Do you remember those dual-control cars in which you learned to drive? Picture the will – your capacity for discriminating judgment – sitting in a dual-control car as the driving instructor, and desire as the student at the wheel. As long as Desire is driving correctly, Will doesn't need to do a thing. But the moment Desire starts to do something dangerous, Will touches the brake, takes the wheel, and says, "That's no way to drive."

Desire retorts, "How do you know what I was going to do?"

"By the look in your eye," Will replies.

When Will is in control, he can tell from the gleam in

the eyes of Desire that what is about to happen is not going to be good for your health, your nerves, and your sleep.

Of course, in the early days, Desire is going to thump on the steering wheel and howl and say, "I'll call the highway patrol!"

But Will just replies patiently, "I *am* the highway patrol."

After a while Desire comes to know that Will is his friend. Thereafter, if there is any difference of opinion, instead of looking upon Will as somebody hostile, Desire will say, "Will, this is something I can't handle." And Will says, "Leave it to me."

This is a perfect picture of the state of balance. It is not that you lose your desires, but your will is always in control. Wherever desire is in control and the will lags behind, there is likely to be trouble – emotional distress, psychosomatic and physical ailments, personal entanglements with painful consequences. These are the problems of energy running out of control. But when will and desire are in harmony, you enter into a state of perfect driving – with power steering, power brakes, power everything. This is victorious living.

★

Living in balance means living in the present, ready for whatever comes.

When I was in my village school, I opened a novel by Charles Dickens for the first time and entered a world that I had never known existed. I was so enthralled that as I got towards the end, I felt so sorry that the story was coming to a close that I would read only for a short while at a time to make it last. My little niece was like that with a candy bar; she was so fond of chocolate that when she got a bar of Cadbury's, she would take just one lick and then wrap it up again and put it aside.

This is all right for children, but it is a little childish for us adults to approach life like this. When our mind treats life like a bar of chocolate, full of pleasure that we can make last and last, it will be looking for chocolate all the time. It will always be restless. That is the root cause of all our hurry. And, of course, a restless mind can't ever be at peace – and how can we expect a mind that's not at peace to find joy anywhere?

When you live in balance, you are in joy always – not joy in the sense that things always take place in the way you want, in the way that pleases you, but in the sense that you are never disturbed and have a quiet confidence in yourself. It is one of the fallacies in our modern approach to life that we believe we can be happy only when everything takes place exactly as we want. Actually, I would say that it's a good thing life doesn't work that way. Sometimes the best things in life are not what we thought we wanted at all, and the unpleasant experiences are what helped us grow.

When harmony predominates, it means your mind is at peace. Then you are a good friend to your friends and a good friend to those who are not so friendly also. When people praise you, you are at peace; when people

criticize you, you are still at peace. You are not any better because of the praise and no worse because of the
censure. This kind of peace of mind cannot be disturbed
by any external circumstance. With it you live in freedom, which is the real fruit of slowing down.

Living in Freedom

T O ENJOY ANYTHING, we can't be attached to it. William Blake understood this beautifully:

> He who binds to himself a Joy,
> Doth the winged life destroy;
> But he who kisses the Joy as it flies
> Lives in Eternity's sunrise.

What we usually try to do is to capture any joy that comes our way before it can escape. We have our butterfly net, and we go after the joy like a hunter stalking his prey. We hide and wait, pounce on it, catch it, and take it home to put on our wall. When our friends come to visit, we say, "Hey, Stu, would you like to see my joy?" There it is on the wall – dead.

We try to cling to pleasure, we try to hug joy, and all we succeed in doing is making ourselves frustrated because, whatever it promises, pleasure simply cannot last. But if I am willing to kiss the joy as it flies, I say, "Yes, this moment is beautiful. I won't grab it. I'll let it go." And I live with a mind at peace and a heart untroubled.

Pleasure comes and it goes. When it goes, we don't need to cling to memories of past happiness or dwell on when it may come again. When we turn to the past in yearning, we are running away from the present. When we propel ourselves into the future in anticipation, we are running away from the present. This is the secret of what the world's spiritual traditions call detachment: if we don't cling to past or future, we live entirely here and now, in "Eternity's sunrise."

★

When I get an opportunity to do something enjoyable – to attend a good play, an interesting movie, a fast soccer match, or game of tennis – I do enjoy it. But I don't let my mind dwell on the event before it happens, and if something requires me to drop my personal plans, I can do so without any lingering disappointment. I'm going to make a tall claim now: I don't know what it is to be disappointed. I have lost the capacity for disappointment. That is a wonderful development, and it comes through training the mind not to have rigid likes and dislikes.

This is nowhere more important than in personal relationships. When we make demand after demand on another person – dictating to them, really, what we like and what we dislike – the relationship cannot last.

In my early days in this country I sometimes had to play "Dear Abby" to members of the beatnik generation, who were as vulnerable as any other generation in matters of the heart. I remember two young people coming to me in private before my talk to say, "We wanted you to know. We are terribly in love." And they looked it: eyes bright, faces smiling. They would sit in front holding hands throughout my talk, looking at each other from time to time with unabashed admiration.

For a couple of months, these two young people would be so fond of each other that they didn't want any physical separation between them. Then, after a while, they began coming in separately and sitting as far away from each other as possible. One would be seated at my extreme left, the other on the extreme right.

"I don't understand," I told them. "You were always together, hand in hand. Why do you now want to be on opposite sides of the room?"

"When we got to know each other better," the girl began, "we realized it wasn't going to work. We're so completely different."

"Are the differences deep?" I asked.

"Yes!" she exclaimed. "In everything. The first day we sat down for breakfast together, I couldn't believe what he was eating. It was like that in everything."

That's how it begins.

"It's true," he agreed. "We just couldn't agree on anything. When we want to go to a movie, she always chooses some romantic drama. I like detective stories, action, but she says movies like that tie her stomach in knots. So we started going to different shows."

These are two people who used to hold hands under the table. Now it's different movies, different vacations, separateness everywhere.

"I have a suggestion," I said. "Would you like to hear it?"

They glanced at one another and nodded.

"I don't think you have any differences at all," I said. "You just mistake your likes and dislikes for deep-seated values. You are not your likes and dislikes any more than you are your clothes."

Their eyes lit up. This hadn't occurred to them.

Then I made my suggestion. "Why don't the two of you go out to dinner together tonight? But don't ask for separate things. Have one person order for both. See how much your differences start to evaporate with just that one little gesture." Then, seeing their faces, I added, "You can take turns. Tonight she gets to choose."

They took my advice and told me later how much they enjoyed making a game of it. I was delighted when they were able to repair their relationship and began sitting together again.

I have seen this many, many times, not only here but in India too. This kind of behavior is universal. Emphasizing differences only makes people move apart. But many of these hasty separations can be avoided when each person learns to like what the other likes.

Even the most cherished preferences often amount

to very little. They are written on water, not on stone; they can be changed. I call this "juggling with your likes and dislikes": turning your preferences upside-down in order to move closer to other people instead of farther apart.

Often, rigid likes and dislikes are merely a matter of attention getting stuck. We get caught in a groove of what we have been conditioned to like or dislike, and we can't imagine getting free. And when we find that others have their attention stuck in their groove, friction results.

Usually, without thinking, we react negatively and move away. But we can learn to play with those likes and dislikes instead, and once we taste the freedom this brings, we really find it enjoyable.

Suppose you and your partner are trying to decide what to do on Saturday night. You have been looking forward to seeing one of the classic films of your favorite European director. But she likes live theater and wants to see a local production of *As You Like It*, though she knows Shakespeare bores you silly. You have been looking forward to your movie; she has been looking forward to her play. What are you to do?

When Saturday arrives, you might say firmly, "I'm going to see my movie." She will say just as firmly, "Fine, then; I am going to see my play." If you are caught in these rigid choices, you are not only not going to spend Saturday night together, you will gradually find you spend less and less time together doing anything. You get used to doing what you want, and if you are rigid in one thing, you are going to be rigid everywhere else. Rigidity is a habit of mind, and if left to its own it will grow more and more unyielding.

But if you want to free yourself from being dictated to by your own habits like this, you can turn your attention away from your film and accompany her to *As You Like It* instead. You'll miss your movie, but you will gain her appreciation.

You don't like Shakespeare. You don't like blank verse. You detest ballads. But you go, and you give it your complete attention too. I have seen people dragged to the theater to please their partner; they can't pay attention, so they sit through three acts thinking about something else. Of course, they have a miserable time. But that's not what you do. You give all your attention to the play, trying to follow the language, and after a while your interest gets caught – perhaps by those glorious words:

> All the world's a stage,
> And all the men and women merely players.
> They have their exits and their entrances,
> And one man in his time plays many parts,
> His acts being seven ages. . . .

"Hey," you say, "this is rather good."

You have never been able to pay attention to Shakespeare, and now you're getting interested – just because you wanted to move closer to a lover of Shakespeare. At the end of the play you admit, "You know, I really enjoyed myself. Honestly!"

Your partner, who has never shown any interest in your European films, thinks, "Well, he *has* been generous . . ." And aloud she says, "Next Saturday, let's go see that movie you've been talking about so much – you know, that European fellow."

★

There are many other benefits of wearing our likes and dislikes loosely. If we can become less rigid in things like films and food, we will be freer in other areas too. We will find it easier to face a task at work which we don't like but which must be done. At times when things don't go as planned, we will be less likely to get frustrated and disappointed. And, most important, we can work more easily with people we don't like.

Please understand that I am talking here about likes and dislikes, not about questions of value. There are legitimate, important distinctions we make every day – for example, between real food and junk food, or between healthy and unhealthy lifestyles – which are not questions of likes and dislikes. The confusion comes because it is easy to confuse what we like or dislike and what is right or wrong.

In Berkeley in the sixties, for example, I was surprised to see that many people with otherwise sound judgment got emotional about hair. Hair was a philosophical issue. It divided generations. You could tell whom to trust and whom to be suspicious of simply by the amount of hair they had – or so, at least, I was told.

I found it difficult to take this seriously. The only

time hair had taken on philosophical proportions for me was when my first gray hairs appeared – and then when they all, gray or black, began to recede.

"All this must look strange to you, coming from another country," one of my colleagues at the university observed. "What do *you* think of long hair?"

I just laughed. "To me," I said, "long hair is long hair and short hair is short hair – and no hair is no hair."

He had the grace to laugh, and I think it opened another perspective for him. Long hair or short hair lies in the realm of likes and dislikes; it has nothing to do with the kind of person who wears it.

Unfortunately, what we like is easily confused with what is best for everyone. The difference is really between what is pleasant and what is of lasting benefit. Pleasure is fleeting; a real benefit lasts. Sometimes, it is true, they coincide. What is pleasant *can* be beneficial. But usually this is only with something simple, such as a glass of orange juice. Most of the time, we need to scrutinize the credentials of any experience that promises to please us and ask: "What are the long-term effects of this experience? What are the costs – not just in dollars but in calories, security, relationships, or self-esteem?"

Again I can turn to films for an example. I have always enjoyed movies, but it is more and more difficult to find anything I want to see. Films made for Hollywood's idea of a family audience are often vapid, and even in a film with a good story, good acting, and beautiful cinematography, I never know when people on the screen will start shooting each other or taking off their clothes.

But even this kind of film is hard to find among the hundreds that are filled with excessive, graphic displays of violence. It is not merely that I do not enjoy movies like this; I don't approve of what they do to my mind. Everything we take in through the senses leaves an impression in consciousness, and the sum total of our consciousness is who we are.

Once again, the Buddha had a very practical touchstone for questions like these. In his eyes, everything we do shapes the kind of person we are becoming. So he says, "If an experience calms your mind, slows you down, makes you more likely to be compassionate and kind, that experience is beneficial; you can enjoy it. If it agitates your mind, speeds you up, excites your senses, or makes you angry or resentful, it is not beneficial; you should avoid it."

★

Likes and dislikes come in the way of love – especially with children. If you tend to be rigid, you may expect your son Joey to enjoy what you used to enjoy. But Joey might have ideas of his own, and enjoy things that leave you cold. To understand him, you have to learn to loosen your own personal preferences and expectations. Then you can enjoy, if not the things he enjoys, at least his enjoyment of those things.

When children want to see a movie that is made for

CHAPTER FIVE

children, many parents take them to the theater, give them money for tickets and popcorn, and say, "Go on in; we'll pick you up after the show." The children are ushered in and the parents leave, saying, "What a narrow escape!"

If it is a film you really disapprove of, wouldn't it be better not to leave them to see it at all? And if it is a film that you simply don't want to see because it will bore you to distraction – say, *The Pink Panther Strikes Again* – why not be brave and go in with them?

You may not like the Pink Panther; you may not like any panther. You don't like Peter Sellers; you don't like French detectives; you don't like the director or the montage man. But you love your children.

So you go and sit with them. And you don't let your attention wander over to the bowling alley or the golf course or your finances; you watch the Panther with the same absorption your children show.

This is where most of us are likely to lose control over our attention. While the Pink Panther is striking again, a part of our mind is on our savings account. We have some old certificates stuck at a low interest rate and we want to take them out, but there is a penalty of three months' interest. We start calculating – three months' interest is this much; how long would it take to earn that back? How have interest rates behaved over the last five years? By the time we have finished calculating all this, the Pink Panther has struck and it is time to go home.

Instead, if you can hold your attention on the movie

118

just to please your children, something wonderful happens: you begin to see the movie through your children's eyes. You know, Peter Sellers can be good. By the time the movie is over, you find that you've enjoyed it. You've enjoyed it through their eyes. Joey will say, "Dad, you're okay. You came with us and put up with our stuff; now we'll come with you and put up with your stuff."

It is in these little ways that companionship grows and the benefits of each other's experience are shared. After all, trying to make other people fit our likes and dislikes is likely only to make us move farther apart. If we care about a relationship, instead of always trying to force the other person to come our way, we can look for opportunities to go his or her way, which is good for both.

★

Just as we may find that our children don't share our interests, we may find that we don't share our parents' interests. Yet we do want to spend time with them; we don't want to move apart.

A middle-aged friend once confided in me, "I find it extremely difficult to talk with my father, and it saddens me because I want to get closer to him."

"I didn't realize it was so hard for you to be together," I said.

"We don't argue or anything," he said. "We just care about such different things. When he starts to talk about golf, I want to scream. I have no interest in golf whatsoever. Of course," he added, "I would never tell him that."

"Then it's simple," I said. "You don't need to have any interest in golf. What you're interested in is your father. Just listen to *him* and not to the golf."

★

Children, of course, can have very strong likes and dislikes where food is concerned. I have seen children turn their faces away and say, "Icky, icky, icky" when they are served something they don't like. But we older people are not so different. We may not say anything out loud, of course, but inside we too turn away and say "Icky, icky, icky" when life presents us with something we don't like.

Food, in fact, is a very good arena for learning to juggle with these rigid responses. Most people are nutrition-conscious today. We are aware that there is a difference between what is good for the body and what merely appeals to our taste. But we still get swayed by old conditioning when it comes to certain favorite foods.

I can sympathize with this easily. Today I am free of likes and dislikes where food is concerned, but that freedom was won only after a struggle. As a boy, like most Indians, I could not imagine enjoying a meal without hot chilies and spices. It was through Gandhi's example that I began to understand that this isn't a very healthy diet. Immediately, I began to reduce spices and salt. For some time afterward, I confess, my meals didn't taste very good. In fact, they seemed not to have any taste at all. But today, after many years of training, I am free. I can taste my food now instead of tasting only the spices in it, and if I were served a meal of highly spiced, deep-fried food, I wouldn't find it enjoyable at all.

By juggling with my likes and dislikes this way, I have changed my eating habits completely. Today one of my great favorites is asparagus. I consume such quantities of asparagus that the checkout clerks can't believe the amount I buy. Once my friend Laurel discovered that a certain supermarket was selling good asparagus at a really low price, so we decided to stock up. On the way I asked her, "Why does this store sell produce at such a low price?"

"It's a come-on," she replied. "You go in for asparagus and come out with a big sack of other things."

Not me. I came home with a big bag full of asparagus, and I used my own bag, too.

★

The palate is one of the sure barometers of inward weather. When I was suffering through a winter in Minneapolis, there was a big sign over a bank which would say "Sunshine" or (much more often) "Snow" or "Storms Ahead." It's like that with the palate. When your mind is under control, your taste buds will ask politely for food that is good for you. But when you are speeded up, your palate is likely to clamor for its old favorites – and you are going to be much more vulnerable to these demands. In this way, by observing how the mind responds to food, we can get a precious early warning that we are starting to get speeded up or out of control.

This connection between food and the mind is unsuspected today, when people are subject to trifling likes and dislikes every day. There seems to be no end to the division and subdivision of taste. In India, in those days, if I wanted ice cream after a meal, I simply ordered ice cream. At most there might have been two or three flavors; often there was only one. Today I have one hundred and forty-seven varieties to choose from, and it's not enough to want chocolate; I have to decide between possibilities like Dutch, Bittersweet, Super Fudge Wonder, and Chewy White Chocolate Macadamia. (Often I just tell the clerk, "Give me the one *you* like best.") And for coffee I have to specify French Roast, Colombian, Kona, or one of a dozen other varieties. I know people whose whole day is affected when they can't get the coffee they like, made just the way they like it. As our preferences get fractioned finer and finer like this, the range of what we can tolerate narrows to a slit – in everything, because this is a habit of the mind.

In Berkeley, our entire household would sometimes go out for a hot drink before my evening talk. One person would order coffee with low-fat milk; a second had to have it with half-and-half. A third took her coffee black, and a fourth only drank decaf. I myself am partial to *espresso* decaf – and one of us insisted on tea. One evening I suggested, "Why not let one person order the same for everyone?" That is what my mother did.

When Christine and I were living with her in India, at tea time she would make a big pot of tea the way she liked it, with whole milk fresh from our cow and a little sugar, and serve it to everyone. We all enjoyed it, and it never occurred to us that we should have a special beverage made to our personal specifications.

If left alone, the preferences of the senses get tighter and tighter until finally nothing is comfortable; nothing will please. The room will always be too cold or too hot, the food too rich or too plain. The neighbor's dog will be too loud, and your friends will not speak loudly enough. Nothing will be quite right.

We have all known older people who find it impossible to tolerate any change of scene or routine. They must sit in the same chair, watch the same programs on TV, eat the same dinner, have the same conversations over and over again. Anything new would not fit into their rigid scheme. And they explain, "We're too old to change."

But it is not only older people who get caught like this. I had a friend who found it disturbing to eat in restaurants – not because he didn't enjoy the food, but because they never arranged the service the right way. As soon as he sat down, he had to rearrange everything: the knife, the fork, the spoon, the glass, the napkin. If a salad fork was not provided, he would ask for one, even if he did not order salad. And he would always order a second spoon – I'm not sure for what. He would be visibly nervous until everything was just so. The arrangements, in fact, were much more important to him than the food, which I would have thought to be the first priority while eating in a restaurant.

This kind of rigid behavior is harmless, however difficult it may be to live with. But consider the person who simply must have things his way or lose control completely. I see items in the papers where a fight breaks out because one person is too slow at a green light or takes another person's parking place. Most people would just shrug when this kind of thing happens. Some feel forced to use strong language. But what of the man who pulls out a gun and shoots another man dead over a parking place? Has rigidity gone so far that he simply can't tolerate any violation of what he wants?

Such incidents are still rare, though I am afraid they are becoming more common in our hurried, unbalanced world. But on a smaller scale, this kind of thing goes on all the time. I often see people get upset over a minor deviation from routine.

When I was teaching on my old campus in India, I used the blackboard often, particularly for writing out the key words of my talk for freshman classes. The physics department had the best blackboards, so I got permission to use their hall when it was not occupied, and they suffered me to teach Shakespeare and Milton where only Newton and Einstein could be mentioned before.

Now, I am right-handed, so I always kept my chalk on the right side of the board. And every day I would go in expecting the chalk to be there and find it at the other end of the board instead. Patiently, I would pick it up and put it where it belonged. But I did get a little irritated. I would ask myself, "Why can't these physics people leave their chalk in the proper place?" And at the end of my class I would leave it in the right place again.

This little drama happened every day, to the great entertainment of the students. If they came in and found the chalk left inadvertently somewhere else, they would considerately move it to the wrong end of the board.

Then one day it occurred to me that the physics professor who played the other role in this drama must be doing the very same thing: finding that I had left the chalk at the wrong place for him and having to move it every day before starting his class. Perhaps he wasn't even right-handed.

That afternoon, when my class was over, I carefully placed the chalk where *he* would keep it.

I did this for a couple of days and nothing happened. I thought all was well. Then one day I came in and found the chalk on the right! Instead of leaving it where he wanted it, he was placing it where it would be convenient for me. It was a marvelous illustration of how ready we are to assume that our way is the only way – and how, if we only go the other person's way a little, he will come a little our way too.

★

We can have rigid likes and dislikes about anything from clothes to opinions, but the most practical place to start loosening them is with the senses: our likes and dislikes in what we taste, smell, watch, listen to, and touch.

CHAPTER FIVE

Freedom from the tyranny of likes and dislikes begins with training our senses to want what we approve of and to obey when our judgment says no.

Training the senses does not mean denying them or depriving them. It means educating them not to demand things that will cost us in health, security, or freedom. In training the senses, we don't forfeit anything in life of lasting value.

The five senses – sight, hearing, taste, touch, and smell – are the channels which connect the mind to the outside world, and the study of the interaction of senses and mind is most fascinating. Just as the body assimilates food, the mind assimilates what the senses take in. In yoga psychology, in fact, it is said that we eat through our senses. What we experience becomes part of who we are.

Most of us are careful about the food we eat, but in terms of what our senses eat, we exercise little judgment at all. We forget that we are eating constantly, especially – whether we are reading a book, watching a movie, or listening to music–through our eyes and ears.

I spent a lot of time at the University of Minnesota getting to know the students in the dorms, and that meant watching a certain amount of television. Most of the fare in those days was westerns, all of which seemed the same. They had the same plot, the same shoot-out, the same sunset at the end. After three or four nights of this I asked innocently, "Why do they keep showing the same program each night? Don't they have anything different?"

Everyone said, "This *is* a different program. That was *Gunsmoke*; this is *Bonanza*." That surprised me. "If you have seen one," I said, "you have seen them all."

They probably thought I needed a little humoring, so they said, "Would you like to have a TV dinner with us?"

They unfolded a small table in front of the TV set and proudly brought out some items on a foil plate. Then they pulled my chair right in front of the wild western blaring on the screen and invited me to eat.

I appreciated their hospitality, but I said, "I have had my dinner already, through my ears and eyes."

TV itself is a dinner, though usually an unappetizing one.

Properly speaking, the senses should act as the mind's office staff, the mind's assistants. The mind is the boss, at least in name. But all too often the boss doesn't boss, and the senses act as boisterous companions trying to get the mind to have a good time. "Hey," the eyes say, "take a look at this new red sports car. Isn't it terrific?"

The ears say, "Studio quality audio – just listen to the sound!"

Touch says, "See how soft the upholstery is!"

Smell says, "Don't you just love that new car smell?"

Taste, for once, is a little at a loss, but he finally steps forward and says, "Great! Let's get in and go get some pizza."

Often all these five characters talk at once. In fact, very often they don't even agree; they are trying to get the mind to pay attention to different things altogether. That is what happens if we eat a good meal and watch a movie at the same time. No wonder we feel confused! And with all this ruckus, who has a chance to hear the still, small voice within?

To enjoy life in freedom – to "live intentionally" – we have to train the senses to listen to us, for the simple reason that attention follows the senses. To do this, it is not necessary to deprive ourselves of good food or good entertainment, but simply to enjoy what is beneficial and ignore indulgences we will regret afterwards.

In fact, what I call "right entertainment" can play an important role in slowing down. I take time to see a good play or movie when one comes around. And when I go, I always go with friends and we enjoy ourselves thoroughly.

I still enjoy going to Berkeley, for example. I moved from the city to the countryside some years ago, but I like to visit the campus, have a good dinner with my friends, and take in a play at the Berkeley Repertory Theater. This kind of outing doesn't require much money; the most important part is the company. We stroll the streets, visit a really good restaurant if we can find something reasonable on the menu, observe the people, enjoy the atmosphere and the scene.

One afternoon we went to Chez Panisse for pizza – an elegant restaurant with lower prices at lunchtime – and then to a film version of a play by Oscar Wilde, *The Importance of Being Earnest*, in a quaint old theater on

University Avenue near Shattuck. This theater is a Berkeley landmark, and its antique seats and faded glory remind me of theaters in India. It is patronized mostly by the campus crowd, who come to see films as classic as the venue. I'm still very much a university man, and it warmed my heart to see students pouring in with their books and papers so they could get a little more reading in before the movie began.

The Importance of Being Earnest is a sophisticated play with a good deal of philosophy behind its humor, and the Berkeley audience showed proper appreciation, lifting the roof off at the right places. The play captures the foibles of the idle rich, which have drawn the attention of playwrights like Bernard Shaw and Noel Coward, and in this play Oscar Wilde, too, is laughing at them in his own light-hearted way.

Lady Bracknell, for example, is examining the suitor to her daughter's hand in the old English tradition. She asks him imperiously how much he has, and he replies with facts and figures that leave her suitably impressed. She also asks a question that might be asked today: "Do you smoke?"

The young man is taken aback, not knowing the answer she wants. Finally he replies, "Yes."

"Good," Lady Bracknell says approvingly. "I like everybody to have an occupation."

The Berkeley students really enjoyed digs like that. But the line that got the biggest laugh was when one of the characters observes, "The very essence of romance is uncertainty." It brought down the house, because all students know that feeling: "Does she or does she not? Does he or does he not?"

It doesn't take any great effort to enjoy an afternoon and evening like this with friends. All that is required is the capacity to appreciate what life has to offer – and not being in a hurry.

★

When the senses are trained, they are alert and sensitive. There is a sense of freshness and newness about everything. Instead of feeling you are in the same old groove, you find choices to be made all the time.

In other words, the kind of life I am talking about is not a life bleached of color. It is just the opposite. I don't think I have ever known anyone who enjoys life more fully than I do, ups and downs alike. Everything that is good, everything that is wholesome, everything that is beautiful can be enjoyed. What is important is that we not cling to it, but enjoy it as part of a life that is lived for a goal higher than our own personal pleasure.

One of the main difficulties in grasping this is that we don't have anything lofty to compare with the humdrum pleasures of sensory experience. Until we have tasted something higher and longer lasting, it's hard to understand what spiritual figures in all ages keep trying to tell us: "Permanent joy is far, far higher than pleasure that comes and goes."

Unfortunately, permanent joy isn't part of our lives

passing pleasure is something we are used to, a dependable feature of our human state. When some sensory experience promises to please us, we cannot think of anything else or imagine there could be anything higher. We get into a fever of longing until we get whatever it is that we want. Only then does it turn out to be not so important after all. I remember a line from James Thurber that captures this perfectly, something about "peach ice cream just not tasting as peachy as it used to."

It is human nature to go after passing sensory gratification. We want it, and want it, and want it . . . until we get it. Then we are likely to find that it isn't as peachy as it used to be, and it is already gone. Yet we always think the next time it will be peachier.

We can spend a good deal of time and energy chasing these will-o'-the-wisp promises, which life simply cannot deliver. Pleasure promises happiness and fulfillment, which are states of mind. But pleasure is only a sensation, and sensations come and go. The more we pursue pleasure, the less satisfaction we get from it – and the more we want. It is a perfect recipe for increasing frustration, bitterness, and alienation for those who do not learn to say no to the senses' clamor.

At the outset, when senses and sense objects come together, we say to ourselves, "What could be more satisfying than this? What could be sweeter?" We do not know that in the long run this honey will turn to poison. What is beneficial, on the other hand, may be bitter at the outset – a fitness program, for example, or a low-fat diet. It may seem like poison. But after a while, as we begin to enjoy the benefits, we see that what seemed bitter is sweet, for it brings the happiness we wanted all along.

In San Francisco, when Christine and I had business to do in one of those massive old office buildings from the thirties, I was introduced to another marvel of American technology: the revolving door. This particular building had a big, heavy glass door that carried a lot of momentum, and once I got in I couldn't get out. Every time I neared an opening, the door would slap up behind me and push me past; and the harder I pushed to get around to try again, the faster I was pushed around. I thought I was going to be trapped there permanently. That is the feeling: you just can't stop; you have to keep going round and round.

Seeing I was in trouble, Christine called out, "All you have to do is stop."

I stopped, the door stopped, and I was free.

That is what happens when the senses get out of control. The revolving door keeps hitting us from behind – *slap, slap, slap, slap!* – and we keep running faster and faster, not realizing that the faster we go, the more we will be urged to go even faster. In order to get out of the trap, we have to slow down the thinking process so as to get control of it, then begin to change our likes and dislikes so we can get free.

Oscar Wilde says in another play, "I can resist every-thing except temptation." When a friend is yielding to a sensory craving which is going to harm him, it is easy for us to see how easily he could overcome it. "Jonathan," we say, "why don't you just step out of the revolving door? Turn your back on the temptation. Just say no!" Only when these things happen to us do we ex-perience how difficult it is to go against a conditioned craving. We need to allow ourselves a wide margin for mistakes while we learn to resist these old, rigid habits – and to allow our parents, our partner, our children, our friends, and even our enemies an even wider margin for the mistakes they make, too.

I am talking here about what G. K. Chesterton called "tremendous trifles." It is my experience that most of our temptations don't come in titanic proportions; usu-ally they are little, little trifles. There is some drama in fighting a great temptation, where the whole world is watching as if its fate depended upon whether we win or lose. The real challenge is to resist those little crav-ings that nibble at us like mice. While we are looking to-wards the left, a mouse takes a nibble from the right; when we turn to the right, we feel a nibble on our left. We can't even take these nibbles seriously – until we find that we've had a third helping of dessert or an extra drink for the road. Life consists of trifles, Chesterton says, and how we deal with them is the substance of our lives.

★

The Buddha called life a sea because the sea is moving constantly. All the world's great religions remind us that we are sailing on an ocean of impermanence. Every experience is transient. Even this body, with which we identify ourselves, changes from day to day. This body of mine is not the same as it was last year. And what about the mind? In the language of Buddhism, the mind is a process, changing all the time. It is a succession of desires. If we satisfy one desire, another will follow; if we satisfy that, a third will come. No experience can bring permanent satisfaction because there is an unending array of desires, one behind another, stored in the vast warehouse of consciousness.

In this sea of change, the Buddha reminds us, time is passing very, very quickly. It is not a negative reminder. To remember this truth does not take away from the joy of life; it adds meaning to every moment.

Some time ago Christine and I took a group of children to Ghirardelli Square in San Francisco. It was summer and the city was crowded with tourists, so it took a long time even to find a place to park. For a moment I even wondered if we should have gone elsewhere. But I had only to look at the children. To them the crowd was part of the attraction, and they could hardly wait to get out of the car and join in.

We wandered through Ghirardelli for a while just looking into the shops, enjoying the mimes and jugglers, and counting the different languages we heard around us. Distractions and color and noise and confusion reigned. The children were in heaven. While they explored the sights, Christine and I found a bench a little to the side and from there simply watched the crowd.

Eventually we joined the long line in front of the old Ghirardelli Chocolate Factory, which we found crowded with pilgrims in search of the perfect chocolate. If it's available anywhere in the world, it must be available in Ghirardelli Square, and people from as far away as Munich and Tokyo were there to enjoy it. I was watching the crowd and looking around to see what was the great favorite of the day. Almost everyone was paying their respects to the hot fudge sundae. Wanting to fit in, we ordered hot fudge sundaes for the children too. Christine and I shared our sundae with one of the youngest, which meant that we didn't get the cherry, we didn't get the chocolate, we got only spoonfuls of what ice cream was already melted in the bowl. We didn't mind; we were there to enjoy the enjoyment of the children.

At several tables, I saw people actually photographing their chocolate confections. This was something I had never seen. They were like patrons in front of a painting at the museum, or like pilgrims at a temple; there was the same worshipful glow in their eyes. The person with the camera would direct people as if he were on a Hollywood set, trying to get everything just right, from the arrangement of the napkins to the big red cherry on top. But the curious part was that after the pictures had been taken, they were too speeded up to pay much attention to their sundaes. They kept talking about the next attraction: Golden Gate Park, Pier 39, the ferry ride on the bay.

I'm sure we sat at our table much longer than anyone else, but the management didn't seem to mind. We did not want to hurry. We felt no need to rush to be anywhere else. We had everything we wanted right there.

CHAPTER SIX
Taking Time for Relationships

SOME TIME AGO I went to San Francisco with a friend. She needed a little cash for expenses, so on the way she stopped at her bank. "It will take only a minute," she assured me.

I thought this was a little unlikely, especially because we didn't even enter the bank but joined a queue in front. There was a machine there but nobody to take care of her transaction. I asked her about it. She replied, "Wait and see."

Curious, I approached the man in front of us to watch what he was doing.

My friend got an apprehensive look on her face and whispered hurriedly, "Let's not stand so close. He's using his secret code, and he may not want us to see it."

He must have noticed the look of amazement on my face, because as he left he smiled sympathetically and said, "You don't know anything, do you?"

I had no previous experience with automatic

tellers, you see, which everybody takes for granted now. I must say it was convenient for us to get the transaction done in two or three minutes. But I couldn't help but feel sorry that this was one more small incident where technology has replaced the human presence, where being in a hurry has eliminated any time for human interaction. Even the sparse human contact that used to exist between teller and customer has been broken.

★

Whether it is the little exchanges between a bank teller and a customer or the fundamental relationships that shape our lives – our ties to partner, parents, children, friends, and co-workers – human bonds are becoming more and more tenuous in today's world. Partly this is because we simply do not take time for human companionship. Personal relationships cannot be left to chance, especially in a speeded-up world. But even in the midst of distractions and stress, we can learn to shape our relationships if we are willing to take the time to do so.

If we have been slowing down the pace of our life, practicing one-pointed attention, and loosening our likes and dislikes, we should begin to see the benefit of these new patterns in all our relationships. For these are some of the tools that can help us make for ourselves a personal world rich in companionship.

★

In order to re-create a world of personal connections, it is important first to understand just how impersonal the lives of most people have become. We are so used to hearing "modern progress" affirmed categorically that it is good to remember that although we have made important advances in certain fields, we have regressed in other areas that are essential to our humanity. It's a difficult thing for most modern people to accept, but where certain crucial human virtues are concerned, we lag far behind our ancestors.

I concede, of course, that we have made great progress in technology. Certain inventions, such as the telephone, seem so basic that it is now hard to imagine living without them. We forget that, by and large, civilization has managed without them. When Christine and I were living with my mother on the Blue Mountain in India, we didn't have a telephone and we didn't need one either. Perhaps the nearest we came to inconvenience was when an American friend who was traveling in India wanted to call upon us and hunted high and low for our telephone number. When he couldn't find it, he assumed it was unlisted. It didn't occur to him that we might actually not own a phone.

Finally he had the bright idea of going to a police station on the Blue Mountain and asking, "Where does Eknath Easwaran live?" The policeman, of course, knew of us and was glad to come to our place in person, bringing our American friend.

What I am saying is: Yes, telephones can be useful; they are not fundamental. Autotellers, telephones, fax machines, and computers are unquestionably useful; they are not fundamental. I talk about computer illiteracy from personal experience because I am one of its victims, yet I do not try to discourage use of computers or other modern conveniences. I am simply emphasizing that compassion, kindness, good will, and forgiveness are the real essentials of life. It is qualities like these that are fundamental to living as a true human being. And that is where our age lacks a great deal.

There is a place for mechanization; there is even a place for automation. But our modern way of life touts mechanization for the sake of the machine and automation for the sake of automation, and everything for the sake of speed. I see everywhere the rapid advance of these forces that strike at our humanity, corrode our sympathy, and make us almost like machines in a world of machines.

★

I am in a special position to illustrate both sides – the human versus the mechanized, the loving versus the hurried – because I come from a world where life was rich in personal relationships, from the richest person to the poorest, the most educated to the most illiterate.

I am not idealizing India. India has many problems. But there is a bright side too, and part of it is this richness of personal relationships.

I grew up supported by intimate relationships. I lost

my father rather early in life, but in my ancestral family, which is matrilineal, the day-to-day influences on my early life came from the women, and particularly, of course, from my grandmother and mother. The three of us were always together. I must have been asked many, many times by relatives and friends, "Don't you want to come to Palghat with us? Don't you want to visit Madras to see a movie and go to the beach?" I would always reply, "I'd rather be with my granny and my mother." I spent every day with them and never grew tired of their company. In fact, I wanted to spend even more time with them.

When I was in high school we had an hour's break for lunch, and the school was about a mile away from my home. Many students used to bring their lunch, but not me; I had to have my meal with my granny and my mother. As soon as the bell rang I would run all the way along the paths through the rice fields, working up a big appetite. When I reached home my lunch would be ready, timed perfectly. My granny would sit on one side and my mother would sit on the other, and there was nowhere else in the world I would rather have been. Nothing was allowed to interfere with this time spent with my family.

It was the same story in the evening. I always wanted to go right home after my soccer game because I knew my granny and my mother would be waiting for me, wanting to hear all about my school day and the game. I related every detail because they were interested in everything. Every friend of mine at school was known to them by name; every play I had made on the soccer field was replayed for them.

It was the same even after I turned sixteen and went away to college, where I did most of the things most boys do at college. When I came home for summer vacation, it was heaven for me to lie on the bamboo cot in the evening and listen to my granny's stories.

This is how my grandmother and my mother laid the foundations of security in my heart. I knew that I came first with them, every day, always, and it gave me a confidence that has withstood every storm life has brought me.

It is not that my grandmother spoiled me. She was a terribly tough teacher. I was not allowed to get away with anything. But she would always stand by me. She pointed out my faults, which were many, and she never connived at what I was doing if she disapproved. Yet under no circumstances would she undermine my faith in myself. This kind of spiritual teaching is a great art, and she was a master of it.

On one occasion she reprimanded me severely in front of my friends, which really hurt. Afterwards, to see if I could make her feel a little sorry for me, I asked her, "Why did you do that in front of my friends?"

She just said, "So it would hurt you well and good."

That was good psychology. I never did that again.

When I was ready to leave for college, she didn't try to dictate my career or influence my course of studies. In India it is common for older people to give strong advice to younger people, and several of my uncles told me in no uncertain language that I should pursue a course in engineering. My grandmother told me simply, "Follow your own star." She didn't try to tie me to her. She said, "All that your mother and I want is that you go out into the world and make us proud that we gave birth to you."

I know that circumstances today in our modern way of life are very different from those that surrounded me as a boy in my village. Yet some things are universal. I believe that our relationships with our children, like all our relationships, can be beautiful. But it takes a lot of time. Relationships require a lot of time and patience: this is what my mother and my grandmother taught me by their way of life. But this simple truth is ignored in our speeded-up world. While appreciating the techno-logical advantages of our modern civilization, let us take time for relationships and cultivate – and help our chil-dren to cultivate – the timeless values and fundamental virtues which make us human.

★

It is through personal relationships that we learn to function beautifully in life throughout its ups and downs. We all need the little human contacts of life, and we all need intimate personal relationships with family or friends. I am aware that many people today do not live with a family, but that is not really the issue. Whether we live alone, with family, or with friends, we can cultivate daily personal relationships. This is pre-cisely where our modern way of life fails us, because it deprives us of the time and the opportunities we need to sustain these relationships.

We can cultivate personal relationships everywhere, in everything, every day. I like to have relationships with each person in my life, even the bank teller and the mail carrier. When I first took up residence in Berkeley, I developed a very warm friendship with the postman. In those days – it seems hard to believe if you don't remember – mail was delivered twice a day. I used to get many letters from family and friends, and after a while their delivery became a personal affair. "Hey," the carrier would say, "there's a letter for you from India today!"

I would tell him, "That's from my mother," or "That's from Meera's mother," or "That's from one of my students." He learned all about my family and told me all about his.

Soon we had a personal bond. He was not just delivering letters; he was bringing me messages as a friend. Once in a while he would say, "I'm sorry, I don't have any letter for you." Can you imagine a mailman saying that today?

On those special occasions when I would receive a package, I would say, "Wait a minute, and I'll show you what this is." I'd open the package and even share it with him, if it happened to be something I could share.

In those days, thirty years ago, a first-class letter cost a few cents. Today, of course, it is several times that, which makes it tempting to conclude that the service must be several times better too. Unfortunately, to put it gently, it is first-class mail but it is not first-class service. Even when it comes to sending or receiving a letter, a human being is superior to a machine. I am supported in this by research which shows that during the last twenty-five years, while machines have replaced people in the postal system, the system has become not only more expensive but less reliable – so much so, in fact, that many of the parcels labeled Fragile are injured in transit. The slogan seems to be "You mail 'em, we maul 'em." I appreciate the hard work of postal employees, but much of their work has been computerized, and extensive mechanization has been put in place. They no longer deliver mail twice a day, and when your package arrives it may look as if it has been run over by a truck. It's a good instance to consider before we accept the doctrine that mechanical operations always make for progress and the machine always makes for efficiency.

At the other extreme is the postal system in northwestern India, a vast desert area with only a few roads, where the most reliable form of transportation is the camel. The camel driver goes from village to village delivering the mail, and since this is an area where many people still cannot read, he not only hands out the letters but reads them for the recipients while his camel has a snack. Often he writes the reply as well! I am not recommending this as an alternative to our own postal service, of course, but it is not wise to dismiss it as backward either. It has a feature totally disregarded or devalued today: it brings people together in friendly personal contact. (You can have a friendly relationship with the camel, too.)

We can reverse the tendency of our civilization to impersonalize everything by making more personal each event in our day. Take the institution with which I began this chapter: the bank. People are likely to say "What does it matter whether you have personal relationships at the bank?" It is simply a business transaction, and the quicker it can be conducted, the better. But these transactions do not have to be impersonal. When I was still new to this country I went to a little bank on Bancroft in Berkeley, and I made it a point to know the people who worked there. I was interested in them, and they became interested in me. After a while, when I entered it was not as an anonymous customer. I would greet them with a smile, and they would ask me what news I had from home. I used to spend a few minutes chatting with the people there and got to know them rather well.

But things didn't begin that way. On my first day there I made out a check in the Indian style, writing the word "Self" where it says "Pay to the order of." The teller had never seen a check like that, and she turned to the others as if I didn't exist and said, "This guy doesn't know how to write a check."

I laughed along with everyone else. Then she came to hand me the money and gave me quite a bit more than I was entitled to. I said to her, "This is a good bank. Here is a customer who doesn't know how to write a check and a teller who doesn't know how to count the money!" She laughed, a little embarrassed, and after that we were friends.

All this banter makes for relaxation. Even now, despite the convenience, I never deal with autotellers. I like to talk to a human being.

At our little local bank on the Blue Mountain, Christine and I would go in and chat with the management about the state of the world whenever we had business there. Once one of our friends in America sent us a handsome check, all of fifty dollars, which I took to the bank. The manager examined this check and found that he didn't have sufficient funds on hand. He had to close the bank for an hour while he went around town raising the money. After giving me the full amount, he said, "Please don't do this to me again!"

On another occasion I had walked into town to buy some vegetables at the street market and realized that I needed about fifty rupees. I went to the bank, saw the manager, and said, "I need fifty rupees but I haven't brought my checkbook."

"Oh, that's all right," he said. "Next time you come this way you can give me the check." And he handed me the fifty rupees.

These are not just financial transactions; these are human relationships in which trust and concern for each other can grow. Such personal ways do take time, of course. At my university in India, I would leave a check at the bank when I was going to my class, and at the end of my lecture the cash would be ready for me to collect. Most people would find this an impossible inconvenience. Wait an hour to get a check cashed? I would ask, Why not? What's the hurry? When you know a transaction is going to take a little longer, you simply plan accordingly. The appeal of the autoteller is that we don't have to plan; we can get money at the last minute – assuming the machine is open and is not malfunctioning. Is that gain worth the loss to our humanity? Is anything worth the deprivation of human relationships?

★

Everywhere in this industrial, electronic civilization there are fewer and fewer personal contacts between people, which means fewer and fewer relationships where trust, intimacy, and concern can flourish.

Television, for example, apart from its other draw-backs, has had a devastating effect on human compan-ionship. We say we do not have time to talk to our neighbors, let alone the teller at the bank or the mail carrier; yet the surveys consistently show that we are watching, on the average, five or more hours of television every day.

When people say to me, "We don't have time for all this," I ask, "How many hours a day do you watch television?"

They count and say sheepishly, "Oh, about four."

I just suggest, "Why don't you cut it in half?"

I do not ask people to eliminate television, but only to keep it within reason. I do watch good shows on television, though they are few and far between. But even then I like to watch with my friends. We enjoy each other's company, and we are together not just physically but in spirit too.

However, it is often difficult to find even an hour's worth of good entertainment on television, and we may well find it better to entertain ourselves.

Some of the most entertaining evenings I have spent in my life were on the small college campus in Central India where I began my career as a teacher of English literature. No one had television, of course. My friends and I could have attended a movie in town, but instead we entertained ourselves by holding impromptu poetry readings. On Saturday evenings a few of my colleagues and some of our students would gather together – the weather was warm enough that we could meet on the terrace of someone's home, under the bright stars – and a Muslim friend who was a Persian scholar would recite some verses of Omar Khayyám by heart. Then I would recite the English translation by Edward FitzGerald, which I had memorized for its intoxicating poetry:

> Awake! for Morning in the Bowl of Night
> Has flung the Stone that puts the Stars to Flight:
>> And Lo, the Hunter of the East has caught
> The Sultán's Turret in a Noose of Light.

Such vivid imagery went to our heads; we were intoxicated by the ardent beauty of it. And my Muslim friend would explain the images for us. When the Bedouin get up at dawn to strike their tents and move camp, he would say, the watchman puts a few pebbles in a can and goes through the camp rattling them.

That's the Bedouin way of getting everyone up in the morning. It suddenly made the verse real for us. Then he would describe the towering minarets of a Persian city as an expression of the human spirit mounting towards heaven, so that we could imagine the rays of the sun reaching out at dawn and catching "the Sultan's turret in a noose of light." Those were such wonderful evenings that every Friday after classes, our students would come up and ask, "Can we have another poetry session tomorrow evening?" This kind of warm, personal human contact is what is lacking in the kinds of entertainment offered to us by modern technology.

In order to build the rich personal relationships that make life worthwhile, time alone is not enough. We also need a firm, lasting basis for relationships, which is why I have made one of the points of my Eight-Point Program putting others first. This is the only permanent basis for any human bond, and if we really want successful personal relationships, it is something we have to work hard at every day.

Of course, this is not merely work. Most people find that it becomes quite enjoyable once they learn to put a loved one first.

Once, after one of my talks, a young college student came up to me and said, "You know, until you suggested putting the other person first, it never occurred to me. But last week I actually tried it with my girlfriend and did what she wanted to do. We went to the restaurant she wanted, and I let her order for me."

"Well?" I asked.

He laughed. "It was great," he admitted. "I just kept putting her first, and we had a lot of fun."

Most of us, in moments of candor, will probably admit that we want to be liked by those around us. We like to please and be loved by those we love. And nothing makes us feel so secure as knowing that we have brought a little joy into the life of someone we care about. That is why putting others first can be such a natural, beautiful part of life.

Yet although it is natural, this is one of the first things to be forgotten when we get speeded up. Putting others first is a skill that we master through practice, even trial and error; and the earlier we begin practicing, the easier it is to learn.

I was fortunate as a boy because I had a loving grandmother who taught me not to insist on always having my own way in my personal relationships. All children have innate self-will, and if left to flourish it cannot help stunting their capacity for loving relationships later in life. My granny never spared me on this score and never let my self-will run rampant.

In my early years, of course, I tried to test my will against hers. Don't think I didn't try quite a few times! Sometimes it worked with my mother, too. But never with my granny – not even once.

In India, one of the easiest ways to bring mothers and

grandmothers to their knees is not to eat. Children learn this at an early age. You just say, "Don't want!" and your mother gives in, your granny gives in, and you get your way. I had seen quite a few of my cousins doing this, so I said to myself, "Why don't I try it too?"

One morning at breakfast, I tried it on my mother. She was really shaken. "I made it specially for you," she coaxed. "Just taste it. Once you taste it, you will like it."

In fact, she had prepared especially beautiful iddlis that morning, and the coconut chutney was most tantalizing. There was nothing I wanted more than to eat that breakfast. Except one thing: I wanted to get my way, too.

So I stubbornly pushed my plate away.

My granny came in at that moment, just returned from the temple, and she saw immediately what was going on.

She sat down next to me and began to comment on the breakfast. "These iddlis are like flowers. And look at the special chutney from fresh coconut. Your mother has made it all for you. Don't you want to eat it?"

Again I pushed my plate away.

"All right," she said, "then I'm going to eat it myself."

I wasn't shaken. I said, "Why don't you, Granny?"

She just sat there and ate it all. Not one bite was left! I had learned an important lesson: never to trifle with my granny.

My mother was always softhearted. After a while she said, "I can make fresh iddlis for you."

My granny said, "He doesn't want to eat them." I still

wanted to get my way. I couldn't bring myself to say, "All right, I'll eat them up." I stuck to my self-will and went without my breakfast.

My granny must have done this three or four times, and after that I never bargained about food – never in the kitchen, never at mealtime. That strategy was left out; there was never any confrontation over food. And my grandmother would explain to my mother, "You see, you have to do that with children. That is the way they learn." My mother understood, but she retained her soft heart. She was not like my grandmother. I was fortunate to have both these wonderful women to raise me: my grandmother, who I realized years later was my spiritual teacher, and my mother, who I came to think of as her teaching assistant.

I have related this to show you that I too had my escapades of self-will. All children try at times to get their way like this and bend their parents to their will. My mother always said that I was an angel until I went away to college; but my granny, while she respected me deeply and in many ways had much higher ambitions for me than I could ever have had for myself, knew that I was far from perfect. In her tough but tender way, she taught me over and over to turn my back on my self-will, because she knew that I would be crippled in all my relationships if I carried that habit into my adult years.

Another incident occurred when I was a teenager. Don't think that because we didn't have television, our village was completely lacking in forbidden fruit. One time a show came to the village which was rather like a musical called *Hair* that was popular in this country in the sixties – music, very physical humor, and a certain amount of indecent exposure. People in my social milieu were not supposed to attend that show, but one of my cousins organized a party in secret. Just like young people in this country, because our elders didn't want us to see it, we had to see it. It had nothing to do with the merit or demerit of the show in question: it was forbidden, so we had to go.

Everyone can be worked up like this, and I got worked up too. I was eager to go with my cousin and other friends.

Most of my family slept on the veranda in the hot season, and everyone went to sleep early. On the night of the show I turned in early, too, and waited until my granny, my mother, and my uncles were all asleep. Then my cousin and his friends came, and we all slipped out without making any sound at all.

We attended the performance, which was just awful, and came back around midnight. I carefully lowered myself noiselessly onto my bed, sighed a sigh of relief, and told myself, "I have done it."

My grandmother's voice came to me softly in the dark. She whispered just one word: "*Nishachara.*"

That said it all. *Nishachara* means "those who move about in the night," and it is the word for all the demons of Hindu mythology. Those are the ones who move about at night while others sleep.

Other than that one word, she never took me to task

about that escapade. But I had learned for myself why she hadn't wanted me to go. Later on, when I was a teenager, if she had to tell me not to do something, she felt that since I was past childhood she should give me a reason. I would just say, "You don't have to tell me the reason, Granny. I won't do it." She used to brag to the entire village, "Is there any other boy in this village who will say he doesn't want to hear the reason?"

This is the kind of perfect relationship that comes as self-will subsides. When you don't always insist on your own way, love, trust, and respect come naturally. The greatest relationship can exist between older people and younger people when they share this kind of trust.

★

We expect professional and financial success to require time and effort. Why do we take success in our relationships for granted? Why should we expect harmony to come naturally just because we are in love?

Naturally there are going to be differences when two people are in love. Even identical twins have differences of opinion, and they come from the same combinations of genes and the very same background. Why should two people from, say, New York City and Paris, Texas, expect life together to be smooth sailing?

Even on the honeymoon there are going to be difficulties. All too often one party will write home after the first week and say, "I never thought it would be like this!" You open Pandora's box expecting doves and out come a couple of bats instead. Here the genuine romantics get most practical. They truly want to learn to love, so they say, "The doves *are* there; they're simply hiding. Why don't we get to work and clean out these bats?"

When irritations or conflicts occur in a relationship, my advice is, Don't move away. Don't say, "I am not going to talk to you; I don't want to see you." Instead, that is the time to say, "I am going to get closer to you anyway. I am going to try to put your welfare first."

There is a very close connection between patience, kindness, and love. Yet this word "kindness" is so simple – so humble perhaps – that we seem to have forgotten what it means. It opens a great avenue of love. Most of us can be kind under certain circumstances – at the right time, with the right people, in a certain place. If we find ourselves unable to be kind, we may simply stay away. We avoid someone, change jobs, leave home. But I have found that in life we often have to move closer to difficult people instead of moving away.

On a few occasions I have had to answer a sensitive question asked by a young man or woman in a romantic relationship: "I have taken time to be with this person, and we both want our relationship to work. But things still don't go smoothly. Sometimes we even seem to be moving farther apart."

I reply simply, "Yes, to move closer to others, you do have to give time to the relationship. But you must also learn to put the other person first, at least some of the time."

I believe that it comes naturally to us to want to contribute to the welfare of those we love. But I am enough of a realist to understand that there are obstacles that stand in the way of the free flow of concern and compassion for those around us. If we understand these obstacles, we will be better prepared to overcome them.

In most disagreements, it is really not ideological differences that divide people. It is usually self-will: putting ourselves first instead of the other person. Sometimes all that is required is listening with respect and attention to the other person's point of view.

When tempers run high, of course, we immediately forget to do this. Most disagreements do not even require dialogue; all that is necessary is a set of flash cards. If Romeo wants to make a point with Juliet, he may have elaborate intellectual arguments, but while his mouth is delivering them, his hand is bringing out a big card and putting it in front of Juliet's face: "I'm right!" Then Juliet flashes one of hers: "You're wrong!" You can use the same cards for all occasions, because that is all most quarrels amount to.

What provokes people in a quarrel is the arrogance of these flash cards. Putting the other person first here means the honest admission – not only with the tongue but with the heart – that there is something in what you say, just as there is something in what I say. If I can listen to you with respect, it is usually only a short time before you listen with respect to me. Once this attitude is established, most differences can be made up.

Years ago in Berkeley I was trying to explain to a student why I gave so much importance to putting the other person first. He kept shaking his head and saying, "Man, I just don't hear you." In all innocence, I started over again a little louder. Finally it dawned on me what he really meant: "I just don't *want* to hear you. I don't like what you're saying, so I'm going to plug my ears until you're finished."

When there is disagreement, this is what most of us do. We carry around a pair of earplugs, and the minute somebody says something we don't like, we stuff our ears until he or she is through and we can start talking again. Watch yourself the next time you find you are quarreling with someone you love. It won't look like a melodrama. It will be more like a situation comedy on television – two people trying to reach an understanding by not listening to each other! One person is saying, "What did you do the other day when I asked you to wash the dishes?" And the other replies, "What about you?" Can you imagine anything more ridiculous? They are not trying to settle their differences; they are trying to make sure that neither of them will forget.

To stop this quarrel, simply listen calmly with complete attention, even if you don't like what the other person is saying. Try it and see. The action will be like that of a play. For a while there is the "rising action": the other person's temper keeps going up, language becomes more heated, everything is heading for a climax. But then comes the denouement. The other person begins to quiet down. His voice becomes gentler, his language kinder, all because you have not retaliated or lost your respect.

★

In personal relationships, most of us are far from free. We are always wondering how the other person is going to react. We are always fearing an attack, or a snub, or perhaps just indifference. So we have all kinds of ego-defenses – moats of suspicion, drawbridges of diffidence, walls of self-will, and several inexplicable trapdoors. With all of these barriers, we expect to sit in our citadel undisturbed, the ruling monarch of our realm. But just the opposite is true. In fact, the more defenses we have, the more insecure we feel, because these defenses are what prevents us from moving closer to others.

When we practice giving our best without getting caught up in others' attitudes and reactions, we find that they begin to lower their defenses, too. Little by little, centimeter by centimeter, the walls begin to come down. Then they too give their best to the relationship without anxiety or fear.

If there is just one person in a group who is always on guard, it is natural for everyone else to raise their defenses also. It becomes a reflex. As soon as we see someone who is on guard, we say, "He makes me feel uncomfortable." We retreat into our citadel, draw up the bridge, close the trapdoors, and wait until he goes away. But the secure person, the person who is comfortable with herself and tries to remember the needs of others, makes everyone else comfortable as well.

★

To excel in anything, we have to have patience. But if we want to love, patience is an absolute necessity. We may be dashing, glamorous, fascinating, and alluring – whatever the current fancy may be – but without patience, our relationships will only grow stale.

"Well," most of us say, "I guess that leaves me out. Patience has never been my strong suit." Very, very few of us are born patient. Our age has been called the age of anxiety; I would call it simply the age of impatience. Almost everybody is too much in a hurry to have patience for anything. You see it in supermarket lines, on the highway, on the tennis court, in the schoolyard, in politics, on the bus. Naturally, we have begun to believe that impatience is our natural state. Fortunately, it is love that is our natural state, and patience is a skill that everybody can learn.

There is a close connection between speed and impatience. Impatience is simply being in a hurry. Our culture has become so speeded up today that no one has time to be patient. People in a hurry cannot be patient – so people in a hurry cannot love. To love, we need to be sensitive to those around us, which is impossible if we are racing through life engrossed in all the things we need to do before sunset. In fact, I would go to the extent of saying that a person who is always late will find it difficult to love; he will be in too much of a hurry. A late riser will find it difficult to love; she will always be going through the day trying to catch up.

Most relationships begin to fall apart through disagreements, and disagreements are not settled by argumentation and logic. They are resolved – or, more accurately, dissolved – through patience. Without patience you start retaliating, and the other person gets more upset and retaliates too. Instead of retaliating with a curt reply, slow down and refrain from answering immediately. As soon as you can manage it, try a smile and a sympathetic word.

So much of the richness of life is to be found in companionship that I can not stress strongly enough how important it is to heal bonds that have weakened and to bring freshness back to relationships that have grown stale.

★

It takes some self-knowledge to understand that when we associate with people, we also participate in their mental states. We are affected not just by what people say and do, but also by what they think.

When we are thinking angry thoughts about somebody, we are throwing abstract rocks at him. Sometimes I think a rock does not hurt so much as a harsh thought, because the hurt from a rock can heal much more rapidly. We know how long people can suffer because of resentment and hostility.

Living in a place where people are angry and impatient is living in an atmosphere worse than smog. We are all concerned about pollution of the atmosphere we breathe, but internal pollution is equally dangerous. One angry, impatient person can upset a whole group.

When we associate with angry people, we come home so agitated that we cannot sit and have our dinner; we cannot go to sleep in peace. And we wonder why. In the afternoon we were feeling so calm and composed; what happened to disturb us? Then we remember: we went out with that person who is always negative. When we are with agitated people, unless we are really secure within ourselves, we naturally begin to share their agitation.

Conversely, in a beautiful manner, when we are agitated and want to express our agitation by agitating people around us, we may go by mistake to the house of someone who is calm and serene. Quietly established in himself, he greets us with a smile that seems to say, "You want to upset me? Sure, come in." We go in and start recapitulating the wrongs the world has done us and explaining how we have always been innocent. But halfway we begin to say that perhaps we do sometimes make mistakes; maybe sometimes we do provoke people . . . Our host is not saying anything; he is just looking at us with love and understanding. But by the time the evening comes to a close, we have become calm. When we leave, we don't know what has happened to our agitation. "Is it the meal I had that corrected my bad mood?" It wasn't the meal. It was the loving, patient attitude of our friend: not anything he said or did, but simply his state of mind.

Have you ever known anyone whose mind was so

calm that agitated people found rest in her presence, angry people became forgiving? People who have the skill of putting others first often play this role. Without preaching to others or advising them, the peace of mind such people radiate has a transforming influence on those around them.

★

John Donne said, "No man is an island." That is why selfless relationships lead to happiness, while a self-centered life leads to loneliness and alienation. As human beings, it is our nature to be part of a whole, to live in a context where personal relationships are supportive and close. We all need support, whether in a family context or in the context of companionship among friends. And I believe we can find it, even in our hurried world.

Because of this abiding need, I have made spiritual companionship, too, one of the steps in my Eight-Point Program. In India we have a word for this kind of spiritual friendship: *satsang*. But in India satsang is sometimes understood as applying only to particular occasions when spiritual aspirants gather together with their teacher. For me, it has a wider meaning. When any loving group of people who share high ideals comes together, it is satsang. Breakfast, when you gather together with family or friends, can be satsang. When you share lunchtime in a loving spirit, it can be satsang. In the evening, when the family gets together for shared entertainment, it can be satsang. Last night we watched a comedy from the thirties with a group of friends, and we laughed so much that the tensions of the day were forgotten. Satsang is not something separate from the pattern of daily life.

Spiritual friendships are what the Buddha would have called "right companionship." Everything we do, he reminds us, either adds or subtracts from our own image as human beings. What we give our time and attention to, what we talk about, what we read about, the people we are close to – all these contribute either to a higher image of the human being or to a lower one.

It is well understood today that individuals take on the characteristics of their society to some extent. But it is not at all understood that we take on the characteristics of our friends as well. We even take on the character of those we admire – sports idols, for example, or media stars.

We can seek out the goodness in people. We can seek out what is noble in human character. We can look for goodness and nobility in choosing our friends, in choosing to whom to give our attention and our love. We cannot afford to give unquestioning admiration to a person simply because he or she happens to be prominent in the media. Yet even if we are thoughtful and have a certain amount of judgment, it is not easy to avoid getting beguiled by these so-called stars.

Everywhere we look – television, newspapers, magazines, books – such individuals are played up. They are not meant to be role models. They are simply gifted athletes, musicians, actors, or actresses. But because of the constant attention of the media, and because of our innate need to have someone to look up to, they take on an aura of supreme importance – so much so that I know young people who are more interested in the latest screen star than in their own girlfriend or boyfriend.

Rather than looking to the media for love and inspiration, isn't it better to look around us? If we confuse media glamour with reality, we are going to find it very difficult to love. Whether we realize it or not, we will always be expecting perfection, which means we will be increasingly disappointed, frustrated, and insecure.

★

In my early days of teaching in San Francisco, a beatnik member of my audience once asked, "You are an educated, cultured, enlightened person. Do you believe in hell? Do you believe in heaven?"

"I have seen people in hell," I replied. "And I have seen one or two people in heaven, too."

If you look back upon your own life – at the times when you were filled with anger, when your mind was in turmoil, when you couldn't sleep – you have been a visitor to hell. But in those rare moments of selflessness which come to all of us, when you forget your petty, personal desires in helping your family or community or country, you pay a brief visit to heaven right here on earth.

Gandhi, in whose India I grew up, with whom I have walked, into whose eyes I have looked, always lived in heaven. He was a citizen not just of India but of heaven too. When the people of India were blessed with good fortune, which was seldom, he was immensely happy. But while they were suffering under the burdens of poverty, famine, and the injustices of foreign rule, he lived in heaven because he was able to help relieve their suffering by showing them how to stand on their own feet and resist injustice nonviolently. Heaven and hell are just two states of mind.

My grandmother used to say in her simple language that there are millions of people who suffer because they make demands on life which life cannot fulfill. Even after centuries of civilization, we still haven't discovered that there is only one way to be completely happy, and that is to forget ourselves in the service of others. Our modern civilization has yet to learn this simple secret: when we pursue our own happiness, we only make ourselves more self-centered and more miserable; when we forget ourselves in trying to add to the welfare of others, happiness comes to us without our asking.

When you look around in any country, you are likely to find a few men and women who have this remarkable gift of being able to forget themselves. These are the people who live in heaven. If you ask me why it is that such people are able to forget themselves, I would say that they have little self-will. All their attention is on others, so they don't have attention left over for dwelling on what they want and insisting on their own way. They don't have time to keep asking, "Am I happy? Is the world tending to my needs?" They are occupied only in giving, only in loving.

To reduce self-will like this and live in heaven always, we have to slow down the mind. The faster thoughts are, the greater will be self-will. All negative thoughts are fast. They are going a hundred miles per hour, so of course we can't turn, we can't stop, we have got to crash. But positive thoughts are slow. Patience is always in the slow lane. Good will is never in a rush. And love is actually off the highway, for it is not a stream of thoughts at all but a lasting state of mind.

If you could see into the minds of people who are self-willed, you would see thoughts whirling round and round like the laundry in a dryer, faster and faster. Such people will get angry without any convincing reason – over trifles, over little pinpricks that would be laughable if the consequences weren't often disastrous – all because the mind is racing out of control. And there are physical implications, as I said earlier. When the mind is going too fast, it naturally begins to affect the body, because body and mind are not separate; they work together.

That is why I say, Give plenty of time to your children. Be patient with your partner, your co-workers, and your friends. If the children take up valuable time narrating some after-school adventure, what does it matter? If your partner forgets to inform you that she will be coming home late from work, or is late in picking you up at the airport, your mind needn't race out of control. It is love that is more important – the harmony of the home, the harmony of the workplace, the harmony of your life. Everywhere, take your time, so that you do not give the mind an opportunity to speed up and get out of control. You will find this is vital in reducing self-will, and whenever self-will is reduced, love has to grow. When you keep going faster and faster, there is no chance even to begin to reduce self-will. You can't even be aware that your mind is racing or that you are being insensitive to the needs of others.

Do you remember the scene in *My Fair Lady* when Eliza accuses Professor Higgins of being insensitive? He reacts with utter amazement. "Insensitive?" he replies, if I may paraphrase. "Me? I am the soul of sensitiveness. Consideration is my middle name. Kindness and I are never parted." This is the self-image most of us have: "I couldn't possibly be selfish or insensitive or unkind." And, in a sense, it is true. Most of us are not unkind people; the problem is the racing, speeded-up mind. To be sensitive, we have to place the highest priority on slowing down and giving full attention to what we do and to everyone we live and work with.

As the mind slows down from sixty thoughts per hour to fifty, to forty, to thirty, to twenty, we begin to see people more and more clearly. It is tragic, but even in many intimate relationships people don't really see each other. That is why they are insensitive: they hurt each other, not willfully, but because they simply don't see. In order to see those around us, to understand their needs, and reflect on how we can contribute to their welfare, we need to slow down the furious activity of the mind.

Putting others first is easy if we remember the needs of the whole. We simply have to ask, What will benefit our family most? What will benefit the children most? What will help us to make a contribution to life? If we ask these questions, we shall find we are putting others first naturally – and that our welfare, too, is included in the welfare of the whole.

A Higher Image

*I*T IS SAID THAT the German philosopher Schopenhauer was walking about one night plunged in thought when a policeman, naturally suspicious, approached and asked him, "May I know who you are?" Schopenhauer paused for a long time before he replied, "I wish I could tell you."

This is the central dilemma of our civilization: we are born, go to school, get jobs, get married, have children, grow old, and pass away without ever knowing who we are. And the question we should ask is: "If I don't know who I am, what is the use of anything I do? If I don't know who is doing it, if I don't know who is enjoying life, what earthly use is it?" That is why the Upanishads say that the joy that comes when we discover who we are is a million times greater than all the pleasures the most advanced material civilization could offer.

Every problem we have today, from stress and difficulties in personal relationships to the devastation we are causing to our environment, can be traced to this fundamental lack of understanding of who we are. For this is what is at the root of our lack of a higher purpose. As long as we believe that we are physical creatures – which is what the mass media are dinning into our ears day in and day out – we cannot help trying to satisfy all our needs in physical ways.

As long as I look upon myself as no more than physical, I have an incomplete idea of who I am. This inadequacy is even more fraught with danger than in earlier times because the media reinforce it every day. Almost every movie we see, every book we read, every advertiser we listen to says, "You are incomplete; you will always be incomplete." And then they offer us some ephemeral object or transitory experience that promises to make us satisfied temporarily. Only rarely does someone arise to remind us that we are not incomplete but whole, not imperfect physical creatures, but essentially spiritual beings whose greatest need is simply to discover our real nature.

"All that we are," the Buddha says, "is the result of what we have thought." Our health is to a great measure the result of what we think of ourselves. Our environment is the outcome of what we think we need as human beings. Virtually every aspect of our lives is directly affected by the image we have of the human being. And today, to put it simply, we look upon ourselves as the body. We try to satisfy ourselves by satisfying the body, and the more acute our inner hunger grows, the more desperately we seek. It never occurs to us that the body is only a house and we are the tenants – or, to use a different metaphor, that the body is a kind of car and we are the driver.

The manager of the bank in a small town near us once told me that if people don't see his car in the front of the bank, they think he isn't there. On the following day they ask him, "Why didn't you come in yesterday?" They identify him with his car.

This happens to me, too. My wife and I used to walk regularly at a nearby beach which is privately owned. In the early days, the girls who check the passes never recognized us; they recognized our car. As long as we were in our own car they would wave us through, but if we came in a friend's car, we would have to show our pass. I wanted to tell them, "Please look inside. It's not the car that has the pass. *We* have the pass. We're not our car."

Today it is different. Once we got to know them, they stopped looking at the car. Instead they look at us, smile, and say, "Enjoy your walk!"

In the same way, when our relationships become personal, we don't identify people by the body they happen to drive. We get to know the person inside.

Unfortunately, if we think of ourselves as physical, we may never get even a glimpse of the person inside. We will see only the outer image. To me it has always been a matter of grief that even an intelligent person may not see parents or partner, children or friends, after living with them for years.

★

Many people would agree intellectually that the human being is more than physical. But if you look at the way we behave – at work, at play, in the shopping center, at home, in the theater, on the playground – you will see what our real self-image is. We don't have a high image of the human being. In fact, we have such a low image that books often become best-sellers by telling us what a low type we are. Countless movies and plays become popular by reaffirming this idea that we are no more than physical, only slightly removed from our evolutionary forebears in the animal kingdom.

We are so set in this belief that I find it difficult to convince people of anything else. If I say, "You are an exalted creature, with a spark of the divine within you that nothing you do can extinguish; and you have been granted life in order to give, because it is in giving that we receive," they find it hard to believe. Today, amidst all this conditioning to the contrary, we need constant reminders of our higher nature, and that is why I recommend spiritual reading as one of the points in my Eight-Point Program.

There is no more absorbing reading than the great mystics and scriptures of the world's spiritual traditions, which offer a vast selection from which to choose. There is no need to limit ourselves to just one tradition, either. Every religious tradition has inspiring literature, and by reading widely we see that, as one of India's most ancient scriptures puts it, "Truth is one, though we call it by many names."

My advice is to set aside a particular time every day, perhaps fifteen minutes to half an hour, to read from an uplifting book of spiritual instruction or inspiration. First thing in the morning and last thing at night are both very good times. Even a short period of quiet inspiration in the morning will anchor the rest of your day; and at night, particularly after a hectic day, there can be no better preparation for sleep. (Of course, these are also the best times for meditation. But if you meditate in the morning along the lines I will recommend shortly, you will find that meditation serves the same purpose of refreshing a higher, spiritual self-image.)

If you end your day with meditation, however, I would suggest that you still have a brief period for spiritual reading before you fall asleep. The events of the day follow us into our dreams, and when we watch television at night or read agitating material, we carry those images and that agitation with us into our sleep along with the rest of our problems. Millions of people read popular fiction at night to get their mind off whatever is agitating them, but these stories only add to the images left over from the day. The techniques presented in this chapter offer a much more effective way to fall asleep with a calm mind, so that we sleep refreshed and awake with spirit renewed.

★

We are so physically oriented that only seldom do we have a glimpse of the pulsating world within us – the world of thoughts, feelings, urges, and desires. This is a world unto itself, a world that never sleeps, never rests. It is the world of the mind.

Physically, at least, we are able to rest a little every night. But mentally we are seldom at rest. The body sleeps but the mind never. This has enormous practical consequences, for a great deal of our vital energy is consumed by the mind. The faster the mind races, the more gas it consumes. When we wake up feeling that we do not have enough vitality, enough drive, enough joy of living to make it through the day, we are probably victims of an energy shortage. This happens to millions of us because we don't know how to minimize the continuing energy consumption of the mind – not only while we are awake, but while we sleep as well.

The most practical and immediate tool we can use to slow down the mind is what in India is called the *mantram*. The mantram, or Holy Name, is a spiritual formula with the immense power to slow down the speed of the mind and lift its attention from any problem that is troubling us. At the same time, it helps to fill our consciousness with a higher image of who we are. The mantram is a living symbol of the profoundest reality we can conceive of, the highest power we can aspire to and love. When we use a mantram, we remind ourselves of our true nature and hold before our mind's eye this highest image of ourselves.

The mantram is an effective brake on the speed of the mind. When the mind is racing in anger, anxiety, worry, or greed, we can use the mantram to slow it down – a skill that is every bit as essential for secure living as good brakes are for safe driving.

In India we had an official called the brake inspector, who was authorized to stop any car on the road and demand to see how well the brakes worked. If you did not prove to him that you could stop your car in a reasonable distance, you would have to have your brakes repaired.

With the mind, too, we need some kind of inner inspector to see whether there is any brake on our anger. Usually he will be forced to say, "You don't have any brakes at all! How do you manage to drive?" Then he will give a citation, because a mind without a brake is a source of danger to us and to those around us too.

If you have power brakes, when you encounter a dangerous situation while driving you have only to touch the pedal to stop the car. Similarly, when your mind is beginning to race – beginning to get angry, to get afraid, to get greedy – you are entering a danger zone where you need some kind of power brake to get your mind under control. That is what the mantram can do.

Repetition of a mantram is a dynamic discipline that gives access to inner reserves of strength and peace of mind. Every one of us has these deep inner reserves; we simply do not know how to tap them. The mantram gives us a way to regain our natural energy, confidence, and balance.

Every religion has a mantram, often more than one. But if you have no affiliation with a religion, you can still use a mantram and benefit from it. I have heard countless times from confirmed skeptics and agnostics – to their surprise but not mine – that the mantram came to their help just when they needed it, though they hadn't expected it to mean anything to them at all.

One of the oldest and most popular mantrams in India, *Rama*, is the one Mahatma Gandhi used. *Rama* (the word rhymes with *drama*) is a name of the Lord that comes from a word meaning "joy" or "to rejoice," so repeating *Rama, Rama, Rama* is calling on the source of joy in our hearts. When someone comes to me for a mantram and says that he or she doesn't believe in God or belong to any particular religion, this is the mantram I most often give to them. It is short, rhythmic, easy to remember, and powerful. Another mantram I often give such people is the Buddhist *Om mani padme hum*. *Mani* means "jewel" and *padme* "lotus"; together the words mean "the jewel in the lotus of the heart." This mantram simply means that the Buddha-nature, a jewel beyond price, is present in every heart.

The Catholic tradition has a beautiful mantram in the simple words *Ave Maria*, which call upon God as the Divine Mother. In the Eastern Orthodox traditions, variations of the Prayer of Jesus – "Lord, Jesus Christ, have

mercy on us," or simply *Kyrie eleison* – have been used as
a mantram for centuries. And for Christians of all traditions, the very name of Jesus is one of the oldest of mantrams.

Similarly, in Islam, the name of Allah itself is a mantram. One of the most popular is *Allahu akbar,* "God is
great." In the Jewish tradition there is *Barukh attah
Adonai,* "Blessed art thou, O Lord," or a revered formula
used as a mantram by the Hasidim: *Ribono shel olam,*
"Lord of the universe."

Whatever mantram you choose, repeat it to yourself
silently, in the mind, whenever you find yourself getting
agitated or speeded up. That is when you will discover
its power. When you have a quarrel with somebody at
work, for example, you have to deal with the situation
somehow, so what do you do? No amount of telling
yourself "I really shouldn't get angry over this little incident" is likely to slow down a mind that is already in turmoil. That is the time to use one of the simplest
strategies which is taught in all the great religious traditions, but which the modern world still doesn't know
about. Instead of reacting with hostility or sitting in silence while your mind seethes with anger, simply repeat your mantram silently until you feel calm again.

This is particularly effective when you can combine it
with a good, fast walk. Just a turn around the block or
up and down a flight of stairs helps greatly. But when
you can manage it – and it's easier to fit in than you may
think – go out for a fast walk of fifteen minutes or more,
repeating the mantram in your mind. When you are

angry or afraid or in the grip of some compulsive urge, when your thoughts are racing and you feel if you don't get your way you will explode, go out for a long walk repeating the mantram for all you are worth. This is one of the easiest methods of reducing the speed of the mind. There is a close connection between the rhythm of the mantram, the rhythm of the footstep, the rhythm of breathing, and the rhythm of the mind.

Repeat the mantram when your mind is getting speeded up by any compulsive urge or negative thought. Ordinarily, to take a small example, when we pass a pastry shop the mind starts to repeat "danish, danish, danish" with greater and greater urgency. Many times, even if we have had our breakfast, we find ourselves coming out of the shop with a little white bag. That is the time to start saying *Rama, Rama, Rama* in our mind. For a while, the mind may try to continue with its "danish, danish, danish." We will be thinking *"Rama, Rama, danish, danish."* Sometimes Rama will win and sometimes the danish. But if we keep at it, the day will come when as soon as we see a bakery, the mantram will start upright on cue, without our prompting. Our mind won't start to speed up at all – and so long as our mind remains calm, we can make choices in freedom wherever we are.

Select your mantram carefully. For some people, the mantram from their own faith comes naturally. The Russian Orthodox tradition has a mantram, *Gospodi pomilui,* that is hallowed by long tradition, and if a person of that faith were to come to me for advice, I would surely suggest that mantram. But there are other people who are allergic to the religion of their childhood. Such people should choose one of the other mantrams I recommend, one that appeals to them and has no unpleasant associations. If no mantram is more appealing to them than any other, I suggest *Rama*. You can never go wrong with *Rama*.

But whatever mantram you choose, don't go just by the sound of it. Try to understand the meaning of the mantram. If in doubt, you'll find that a short mantram is easier than a long one to call to mind when you are agitated. And please don't make up your own mantram. Use a mantram that has been sanctified by tradition, as have all the ones I recommend here.

Once you have chosen a mantram, stick to it. Don't try one for a while and then change to another. If you do, you will be like a person who keeps digging wells in many places; you will never strike water. Instead, use your mantram as much as possible – silently, in the mind – whenever you find an opportunity: while waiting in line, while doing mechanical tasks like washing dishes, and especially while falling asleep at night. Practice – diligent, determined practice – is what counts with the repetition of the mantram. At first the repetition may seem mechanical, but every repetition takes you a little deeper. Gandhi used to say it's like walking: each step is like all the others, but you are moving forward with every stride.

Of course, when you are doing a job that requires attention, you should not try to use the mantram. That is the time to give your complete attention to the job. Most work requires this kind of attention. When operating a piece of machinery, one-pointed attention is not just training the mind; it is vital for safety. (Driving, incidentally, is operating a particularly dangerous piece of machinery.) These are not times for the mantram. But there are many, many occasions during the day when the mind is not actively engaged in a one-pointed task, and those are just the times when it tends to get caught in old, compulsive habits – worry, resentment, insecurity, gossip, replaying old tapes from the past. Similarly, a great deal of talking is not really necessary; some of it is even compulsive. These are all times to use the mantram instead.

Whenever I get a few moments here and there, I use the mantram. I pick up stray moments like a miser picking up a penny. When I ride in a car, I hardly talk because I am repeating the mantram in my mind. When I go for a walk on the beach I repeat my mantram. When I am seated without anything in particular to do, I repeat my mantram. When I am going to sleep, I repeat my mantram. With any skill, whether it is tennis or the mantram, this is the story: practice makes for success.

We can use the mantram to invigorate the mind when we are getting bored, and to overcome inertia when we feel physically or mentally stale. And we can use it to control restlessness when the mind is speeding up. The mantram is an indispensable tool that I recommend to anyone who wants to find balance in a world of stress and hurry. If you would like to read more about it, there are a great many more suggestions and examples in a book of mine called *The Unstruck Bell*.

★

In 1960 I began a series of talks in a bookstore on California Street in San Francisco, where I drew a good number of beatniks. I was waiting for a chance to introduce meditation, but in those days even beatniks were unfamiliar with this subject, so I kept my talks on a philosophical level. But the audience seemed idealistic and sincerely interested, so one day I said to myself, "These are bright people, and some of them have been asking really searching questions. Why don't I teach them how to meditate?"

That night I gave complete instructions to a full house. Meditation, of course, is one of my favorite topics, and my audience responded to my enthusiasm with keen attention. At the end of my talk I said optimistically, "All right, shall we meditate now?"

We all closed our eyes, and I got absorbed. When I opened my eyes thirty minutes later, there were only three people in the room – my wife, myself, and the owner of the bookstore, who was waiting to lock up.

That is when I realized it was going to be extremely difficult to teach meditation in this country.

I have great sympathy with people who find it hard to meditate. It *is* hard. In the Bhagavad Gita, taming the restless mind is compared with trying to tame the wind. Nevertheless, I know of nothing on earth that can remotely compare with the benefit that even a little practice of this powerful discipline brings.

In the last thirty years, I have learned a great deal about how to present meditation so that it can have maximum benefit in our modern way of life. My instructions are based on my personal experience and addressed to people with some experience of life who have tasted some of its fruits and thirst for something more. Meditation is the basis of a life of splendid health, untiring energy, unfailing love, and abiding wisdom. It is the very foundation of that deep inner peace for which every one of us longs. No human being can ever be satisfied by money or success or prestige or anything else the world can offer. What we are really searching for is not something that satisfies us temporarily, but a permanent state of joy.

★

This word "meditation" is used today in many different ways. The only method I teach is the one I have followed in my own life, which I have presented to thousands of Americans over the last thirty years. It has two important aspects. First, of course, it slows down the mind, making it increasingly calm, steady, and clear. It does this by sustained attention on a single focus: the words of an inspiring passage that embodies a lofty ideal.

The second aspect is less obvious: since we are what we think, we become what we meditate on. The sustained attention we give to our meditation passage drives it deep into our consciousness, so that the ideals it embodies gradually become part of our character and conduct.

Obviously, it is important to choose such passages with care. They must be positive, practical, universal, and inspiring. They should reflect authentic spiritual experience. And they should present the highest possible image of the human being.

All the passages I recommend for meditation are chosen from the world's great religious traditions, and they are universal as well. They embody the conviction that God is not to be found outside us, and that a spark of the divine is present in every human heart.

Because this conviction is found in every major spiritual tradition, using passages from different sources is like looking at Mount Everest from many different perspectives. You get one view of the Himalayas from India, another from China, a third from Pakistan, a fourth from Bangladesh, a fifth from Tibet. But these towering peaks are always the same, like the power that is present in each of us as our real Self.

You will find a rich collection of passages for meditation in my book *God Makes the Rivers to Flow*. I recommend beginning with the beautiful Prayer of Saint Francis of Assisi:

Lord, make me an instrument of thy peace.
Where there is hatred, let me sow love;
Where there is injury, pardon;
Where there is doubt, faith;
Where there is despair, hope;

Where there is darkness, light;
Where there is sadness, joy.

O Divine Master, grant that I may not so much seek
To be consoled as to console,
To be understood as to understand,
To be loved as to love;
For it is in giving that we receive,
It is in pardoning that we are pardoned,
It is in dying to self that we are born to eternal life.

I don't think anyone has ever presented a loftier image of the human being.

If you meditate every day on the words of Saint Francis, you will find yourself gradually becoming a little more like him. Wherever you go, you will bring a little more peace, a little more hope, a little more love.

★

The best time for meditation is early in the morning – as early as you can reasonably make it. There is a wide margin for personal circumstances, job requirements, and family situations, but in general, the earlier the better. In a tropical country like India, the auspicious hour for meditation is in the small hours of the morning when the land is still cool and the breeze still fresh. Here it is not necessary to meditate so early, but by and large, it is good to get started by six o'clock.

When I said this in my meditation class on the Berkeley campus, I was greeted by sighs and groans. I thought six o'clock was reasonable, even lenient. But most of them found it untenable, because they liked to stay up late – sometimes until two or three o'clock – discussing the nature of their subconscious in the crowded coffee houses of Telegraph Avenue. I suggested, as a practical measure, that if they wanted to bring their lives into closer harmony with the rhythms of nature by getting up early, it would help a great deal to go to bed early – say, by ten or eleven o'clock.

If you are used to having a cup of tea or coffee when you get up, there is no need to eliminate it now. Gradually you will not have the need for caffeine, and in the long run it is not very helpful to add stimulants to the nervous system when you are trying to slow down. But it is much better to have a cup of tea or coffee and then sit down to say "Lord, make me an instrument" than to have your deprived mind keep saying, "Make me . . . a cup of tea."

If you feel particularly lethargic at six in the morning, you might try going for a short, brisk walk repeating your mantram. If you are used to having your run in the morning, you may do so before meditation, but do keep repeating your mantram while you run. Come back refreshed and ready to meditate. You have been warming up for the greatest exercise in the world: the training of the mind.

I learned to meditate in the midst of an extremely busy life at a large university in India, where I had many cultural interests and responsibilities from early morning until late at night. So when somebody comes up after one of my talks to say, "I would like to learn to meditate, but I don't have time," I don't take it too seriously. I know from personal experience that everyone can find half an hour a day, especially for something so rewarding.

★

Choose a place for meditation that is quiet, clean, cool, and airy. If you have a small room that you can devote to this purpose, you will find that is a great advantage. If you cannot have a room, set aside a special corner. Whichever you choose, reserve that place for meditation and spiritual reading only. Don't discuss other topics there; don't read other books there; don't use that place for any other activities. Gradually you will associate that place with meditation just as you associate the den with watching TV or the dining room with eating. Then you will find that simply going into your meditation room will begin to calm your mind. Your family will see you going in agitated and coming out serene and secure, and they will absorb the benefit of it too.

If you find it helpful, you may decorate your meditation place with an image of some spiritual figure that you find elevating – of Jesus, perhaps, or the Buddha, or one of the saints. Otherwise, keep your meditation room or corner austere.

Similarly, you don't need any special paraphernalia to meditate. I see catalogs that sell clothes and other items intended for meditation, but it is enough simply to wear clothes that are comfortable and loose. They may not be the mirror of fashion, but as long as your body is comfortable, they are better than anything you can order from a catalog. You don't need to spend money to meditate; this is just another attempt by marketers to make something simple into something complicated.

Our modern civilization cannot resist the temptation to bring in technology, even where meditation is concerned. I have seen electronic gadgets which are supposed to make meditation quick and easy. I can assure you that if something is quick and easy, it isn't meditation. Meditation is a practice that is meant for our whole life. We don't expect to attain a state of instant fitness and then stay fit for the rest of our lives without exercise. Why should we expect anything different for the mind?

In the early sixties, when the Beatles took to meditation, probably thousands of young people followed their example. I didn't object to that; I was delighted to see so many people meditating. But I had to point out to them that if you take to meditation because your favorite rock stars are meditating, you are likely to stop when they stop meditating too.

★

Next comes the question of how and where to sit. Meditation manuals often recommend what yoga calls the "lotus position," cross-legged on the floor with your feet on your thighs, but that way of sitting is very difficult to learn unless you begin when you are young.

Most Westerners find this an excruciating position from which they may not be able to get up easily. I have seen people attempting the lotus posture, determined not to let it master them. They sometimes remind me of a story about Edward Gibbon, the author of *The Decline and Fall of the Roman Empire*. Gibbon was a rather portly man, disinclined to physical exertion. When he fell in love with a certain lady, he went down on one knee, as was customary in those days, to ask her if he could aspire to the honor of her hand. She replied tactfully that she had other plans. "In that case, madam," said Gibbon, who had a satirical vein, "would you please help me to get up?"

Where posture in meditation is concerned, the most important thing is to choose a position comfortable enough that you forget your body, while keeping your spinal column erect. You may certainly sit cross-legged on the floor, but a straight-backed chair is fine. (Choose one with arms; they help prevent slumping.) Whether you choose the carpet or a chair, you may find it helpful to have some support for your back.

On the other hand, don't make yourself too comfortable or you will fall asleep. Tension comes because the mind is divided; concentration, a unified mind, brings relaxation. One of the first effects of meditation is that your neuromuscular system begins to relax, causing you to feel drowsy. It is important right from the outset not to yield to this tendency. When you feel you are growing sleepy and letting the meditation passage slip through your fingers, draw yourself away from your back support and sit up straight until the wave of sleep passes over.

In the beginning, provide half an hour for meditation. Less than this will not really give your mind time to slow down its usual pace. Practically speaking, it's a good idea to set aside a little longer period in your morning routine so that you don't have to keep checking your watch. You will gradually learn to time your meditation by the length of the passage. I don't recommend meditating for longer than half an hour either. If you want more meditation, add half an hour in the evening.

You may find it difficult at first to sit still for thirty minutes. The mind is a restless creature, and it will do its best to convince you that you simply can't sit there another minute; you have to be up and doing. Teaching this compulsively restless mind to subside is one of the main reasons you are meditating! To make it easier, try going for a brief, brisk walk repeating the mantram before you sit down for meditation. Almost everyone has trouble learning to meditate, but everyone can repeat the mantram, which is one of the very best ways of preparing the mind for meditation.

Just as some people have a natural flair for soccer or mathematics or music, there are a few people everywhere who have a native capacity for meditation. Such people can suddenly break through to a deeper level of awareness. As they get absorbed in the words of the meditation passage, their breathing slows down, which means that their heart rate and other biological functions slow down too. These and other, more subtle changes in the functioning of the body take place as meditation deepens, with beneficial effects that spread throughout body and mind.

★

Now to begin. You will need to have memorized a passage for meditation, such as the Prayer of Saint Francis, and perhaps reviewed it the night before. Enter your meditation room or corner, sit down, and gently close your eyes. Place your hands comfortably where you are least aware of them, just resting loosely in your lap. Then gently close your eyes and start to go through the words of the Prayer of Saint Francis as slowly as you can, letting each word fall like a jewel into the depths of your consciousness.

I say "as slowly as you can" because the usual tendency is to race through the passage, escape from your meditation room, jump into your car, and rush back into the rat race. The mind resists even the idea of slowness, and it is a very clever customer. It knows what you are up to. It suspects that you are trying to deprive it of its independence – that's how the mind regards it – and it objects, "I have my rights: to agitate you and upset you and to go as fast as I please. This meditation business is an unfair invasion of my rights. That you should be calm and kind under all circumstances is nothing less than a life threat to me, and I'm not going to take that lying down."

You can appreciate the mind's point of view. After all,

it doesn't want to become what Zen calls "no mind." But on the other hand, you need to teach it how to behave; otherwise it will continue to drive you around as it likes. So try to slow it down right from the outset. Begin the Prayer of Saint Francis like this: "Lord . . . make . . . me . . . an instrument . . . of thy . . . peace," giving your attention fully to each word.

Don't go so slowly that you leave big gaps between the words; that only invites distractions. But don't rush through the words at conversational speed either. After a little experimentation, you will find the right pace. The goal is for your attention to flow smoothly through the passage without a break, without wandering to any other topic. Then, the Bhagavad Gita says in a beautiful image, your mind will be like the flame of a lamp in a windless place; it will not flicker at all.

For a long time, of course, your attention *will* wander. That is the nature of our conditioning. There is no need to be distressed when this happens. Whenever your attention strays to your job, to the discotheque, to the dentist's chair, to the movie theater, simply bring it back to the words of the passage.

This is a demanding discipline, but it will pay rich dividends. Today, after years of practice, my attention is effortlessly one-pointed all the time. Whatever I am doing, it is like driving from here to San Francisco in the same lane.

Actually, you will never see me driving on the freeway to San Francisco because I don't drive. My American friends always say, "We'll drive. You just sit and repeat your mantram." So I don't have a California driver's license. But I am a fully licensed driver of my mind. I wish you could see me driving the car of my mind – just cruising along. Most of the time I can put my feet up and just roll along on cruise control. You won't see any weaving; you won't see any speeding. I just drive in one lane. And as long as the mind is traveling in the same lane, anger cannot come, fear cannot come, greed cannot come. For all of these negative states, the mind has to change lanes.

It is the nature of the mind to flicker. It is the nature of the mind to wander. It is the nature of the mind to go up and down. Even after the first line of the passage, you may find your attention slipping away to the work you want to do the next day in the garden. One part of your mind is on the Prayer of Saint Francis while another part is asking innocently, "Do you think a red rose or a yellow one would look best in that new bed?" There is no connection at all between this and the words of Saint Francis, but you say, "I don't think roses . . . perhaps a few vegetables." That is just what the mind wants. It wants you to start thinking about something in the past or the future. So it says, "Okay, not roses. Which vegetables, then?"

You have gone through only the first five words of the passage – "Lord, make me an instrument" – and the mind has got you thinking about gardening already. When this happens, don't get agitated; don't get mad at your mind. It likes you to get mad because then it has your attention. Instead, tap your mind on the shoulder and say politely, "Excuse me, but you're not supposed to be here in the garden. You're supposed to be meditating." And bring it back gently but firmly to the words of Saint Francis. If it has wandered from the passage completely, take it back to the very beginning and start again: "Lord . . . make . . . me . . . an instrument . . . of thy . . . peace."

This is language the mind understands. For a while it will groan and complain, "What, again?" But you just reply firmly, "Yes, again. Every time you wander, this is what we are going to do." After a while, your mind will accept the fact that when you sit down for meditation, it is expected to behave – at least for thirty minutes.

As many times as your attention wanders, bring it back. Pay more and more attention to the words of the passage. Don't try to resist the distractions or to push them out; you will only be strengthening them. Instead, simply turn up the volume on the words of Saint Francis.

Once some students complained to their meditation teacher, "Why shouldn't we resist distractions when they come? Why not just push them out of the mind?"

"All right," said their teacher, who had a mischievous sense of humor. "When you sit down for meditation this evening, push out whatever distractions come. But whatever you do, don't think about monkeys."

That night in meditation, those students couldn't think about anything else. Monkeys kept slipping in, through the door, through the windows, through the ventilator, and the more they tried to push them out, the more monkeys came in. Their whole half hour was spent in fighting monkeys.

That is why I say not to resist distractions. If you resist one, two will come; if you resist those two, three will come – simply because you are feeding them with your attention. Instead, just give more and more attention to the words of the passage.

There is a marvelous skill in this that you will develop with practice. Once you have learned this skill, instead of getting agitated and afraid when old memories come, rattling their chains and wearing ghoulish makeup to frighten you, you can sit back and say, "Good show! Are you quite through?" The ghosts of the past will have no hold whatever on your attention, which means there is no emotional connection at all.

Never underestimate the cleverness of the mind. It has all kinds of cards it can play, and aces all the way up its sleeve. It can substitute almost anything for monkeys. Some people, when they start meditating, find that their throat immediately gets dry or their mouth begins to salivate. All they can think about is whether they are going to cough or swallow. If something like this happens, just give more attention to the inspirational passage. Often it helps to keep a glass of water by your side. Oddly, when the mind knows the water is handy, it ceases to nag you about your throat.

My observation, after more than thirty years of teaching meditation, is that most problems are no bigger than that little urge to cough. It is by dwelling on them, brooding on them, feeding them with our attention, that we make them bigger and bigger until they seem to tower over us. Some trivial problem looks as big as King Kong, and we feel no bigger than a mouse. When we learn to direct our attention, it is the problem that is the mouse and we who tower over it.

★

When you reach the end of the Prayer of Saint Francis, you may simply start over again until your thirty-minute period is over. But as soon as possible, I recommend that you memorize other passages for meditation to use as well. If you use the same passage too often, it will lose its freshness. It is good to memorize a wide selection of passages that appeal to you deeply, and to go on memorizing new ones. I still carry a small card with me on which I have jotted verses I want to learn. When I have a few minutes while riding in the car or waiting for someone, I use that time to memorize a verse or two.

Even if you do nothing in thirty minutes but bring your mind back thirty times, you have done wonderfully. You may feel you have wasted your time, but that discipline will go on paying off throughout the day. Over the months, as the bank advertisements put it, it all adds up. Eventually, you may be bringing your mind back only ten times. Then it will be only once or twice. Finally, if you practice systematically and with sustained enthusiasm, the day has to come when you do not have to bring the mind back even once, because your attention never wavers.

I cannot describe to you the splendor of this experience. All your attention is completely integrated, focused like a laser on the words of the passage. Your senses close down and you are blissfully unaware of your body. In this supreme experience you know that the body is not you, but only the house in which you live. You feel a presence stirring in the depths of your consciousness, so healing, so loving, that Saint Francis said that if the experience had lasted longer, his life would have melted away in joy.

Compared to this experience, all the pleasures of the world become insignificant. Even the most elevated artistic experiences cannot be compared with the boundless joy and love we feel in this supreme state. One taste of it, even for a moment, and you will want to make it last forever.

That is why I tell everyone to make meditation their first priority. No time could be better spent. I led a very busy life when I began to meditate many decades ago, and I still lead a busy life, but I have always found time to meditate. You can be sure that when you make meditation your first priority, you will enjoy the benefits from it every day.

Even after decades of meditation I still cannot get over the miracle of what precious treasures lie within our consciousness, ready to be discovered through the practice of this simple discipline. Every morning as I finish my meditation, I realize anew how immensely it can enrich our lives and the lives of those around us.

I think it is important for everybody to learn to meditate. Anybody who wants to be healthy, which means everybody, needs to meditate. Anybody who wants to have a calm mind and a loving heart, which again means everybody, needs to meditate. The reason why more people don't meditate is that they don't have an opportunity to hear what meditation is. From my first talk on meditation at that bookstore in San Francisco, it was only a few years before I was teaching meditation at the University of California to hundreds of students in one of the largest lecture rooms on campus. They were an enthusiastic crowd, eager to hear, longing to learn. This country is full of people with daring and determination, and I have been privileged to teach thousands of them in the last three decades, though meditation was virtually unknown when I first arrived.

One of the greatest benefits of meditation is the loss of any feeling of inadequacy you may have. It is amazing to me, but I don't ever feel inadequate today. I don't know what the meaning of depression is. I have many important responsibilities, many challenges come up every day, but I know that I can dive deep into my consciousness in meditation and bring up with me the resources necessary for dealing with any dilemma the day may bring.

I was not born this way. It is something that I achieved through long years of discipline and the grace of my teacher, my grandmother. And when this state is achieved, a great teacher of meditation in ancient India makes this quiet statement: "Now you see yourself as you really are."

Before I took to meditation, although I was leading a satisfactory and successful life, I didn't have any idea of who I am. Of course, I thought I knew. I was a village boy from Kerala who had become professor of English on a campus in Central India and was sure he was enjoying life and perhaps even contributing to it a little. Only later did I realize that I had been asleep and dreaming – no more awake, as William James says, than a man who thinks his capacities are limited to what he can do with his little finger.

One of the inspired verses of the Katha Upanishad defines clearly who we are:

> When the wise realize the Self,
> Formless in the midst of forms, changeless
> In the midst of change, omnipresent
> And supreme, they go beyond sorrow.

The beauty and wisdom of these words is unsurpassed. They express the summit of human wisdom, because they tell us who we are. They say, in the simplest possible language, that within this physical, changing, mortal body there is a nonphysical presence which is our true Self.

When I was enabled, after years of meditation, to discover who I am, the joy of that discovery knew no bounds. And my love knew – and knows – no bounds. Today I know I am not just a separate fragment of existence subject to old age and death. I live in everyone. I am related to everything around me – the seas, the skies, the mountains, the rivers, the forests, the beasts of the field and the birds of the air. I am an immortal being with a million interconnections with all of life. This is our greatness, to be connected with everything on earth. And when we discover this, as the Katha Upanishad says, we go beyond all sorrow.

CHAPTER EIGHT
The Still Center

ONE OF MY DELIGHTS as a professor of English literature was to introduce Shakespeare to a freshman class. T. S. Eliot used to say that any scholar who claims direct knowledge of Shakespeare is a mythical creature, and this was corroborated in every final I gave. My students almost never told me what they themselves thought about Shakespeare. They gave me only quotations from the experts. If I asked them about *King Lear,* I would learn what Bradley thought about *King Lear.* If I asked about *Henry V,* they would quote Quiller-Couch. If I asked for a précis of a plot, they would use the words of Charles Lamb. I finally came to the conclusion that if I could talk to somebody who had read Shakespeare himself, it would be an exceptional experience. "Don't tell me what the experts say about the play," I would insist. "I've read the experts. I want to know what *you* have learned, what this play means to you."

That is one of the reasons I refer to Mahatma

Gandhi so often. When Gandhi wrote or said something, it was always based on direct, personal experience. This overriding practicality is one of the marks of genuine spiritual experience. Gandhi did not spend time theorizing and philosophizing. He would always say, "Why not learn by getting down to the actual practice?"

Sri Ramakrishna, a great nineteenth-century Bengali mystic, used to say similarly, "When you go to a mango tree, you don't go to count the leaves. Get up into the tree, pluck a mango, and eat it; then you will know about mangoes." When it comes to the benefits of stilling the mind, there is no substitute for giving it a try and tasting the fruits of it ourselves.

★

All of us have moments when we forget ourselves, forget the passage of time completely – usually when we are intently absorbed in doing something we like.

In my early days in this country, a friend of mine took me to see American football, which is entirely different from what we called football in India (you call it soccer). There was a big crowd, and a lot of excitement when those figures dressed in primeval costumes and looking like supermen came onto the field. My friend was a good commentator, and he carefully explained to me the system of scoring and some of the rules of the game. But during the second half of the match he got so completely absorbed that he stopped talking to me. Then, suddenly, one side scored a touchdown. My friend – usually a rather reserved person – jumped up and fell upon the man seated in front, squashing his hat on his head. I told him later, "You not only forgot yourself, but you forgot the poor fellow seated in front of you, too!"

Whether we are aware of it or not, all of us are capable of these moments of utter self-forgetfulness, and it is in these moments that we experience happiness. You can see why I call it a tragedy that we are bombarded with propaganda that tells us to dwell on the body as the source of joy, for joy is to be found in just the opposite direction.

In the deepest stages of meditation, the mind gradually comes to a temporary stop. Then you experience the state that Zen Buddhism calls "no mind." It sounds negative, but this is a tremendous experience. Afterwards, you realize that just as your body is like a car you drive, your mind is the engine. And you are the driver — which means, among other things, that you know how to slow down your car when you like and even how to park it, put the engine in neutral, turn it off, and put the key in your pocket. Most of the time, without realizing it, we leave the mind idling on the street with the key still in the ignition, where it wastes gas and pollutes the air until some vagrant thought drives off with it.

This mind of ours is constantly chugging away, even when it is doing nothing. To be able to turn it off and let it rest without thought is to be in heaven. To have a still mind means there is a healing silence everywhere. In this supreme state, you are absolutely fulfilled. You don't need anything outside yourself. You don't need to manipulate other people. You don't need to accumulate material possessions. You don't need to depend upon any of the unreliable props that modern civilization produces.

This experience of the still mind may last just for a few moments, for the twinkling of an eye. But once you taste this experience, you realize how paultry all the satisfactions of the external world are.

People often ask me, "How would you compare your life today with your life before you took to meditation?" I don't come from a poor family, so I don't answer as someone who was ever deprived. In fact, I come from an affluent, cultured family that has produced leaders, scholars, and artists in my part of Kerala for centuries. I had a good education and was able to pursue the careers I wanted as a college professor and writer. And I enjoyed my work very much. I used to tell my students, "Instead of the government paying me to introduce you to Shakespeare, I should pay the government for giving me the privilege of sharing with you the books I love." By Indian standards, I was quite successful. I had no frustrations – in fact, I was a happy man. Yet today there is no comparison. I am living a million times better. Not just better, a million times better.

Until you have this experience for yourself, you cannot really understand it. But once you get a taste of the love and the joy of it, you will want to live in this state permanently.

★

In the spring, when the weather is beautiful and the hills of California are green with new grass, I sometimes go for a "joyride" in the afternoon with a few friends. I always say to the driver, "Don't go fast. I like to look at all the cows and calves, the sheep and lambs, the deer, the wildflowers on the hills."

This is very much like what happens in your mind when your thinking process is slowed down through meditation. Then you are able to see thoughts with some detachment. You can see them gamboling like lambs on the hillside, and if they are playful and beautiful like the lambs, you can enjoy them. You can see even the small, tender thoughts that grow like wildflowers in out-of-the-way places. Life becomes most enjoyable.

Of course, unpleasant situations still come. No one can avoid them. But when your mind is still, instead of getting agitated in an unpleasant situation, you can see the other person's point of view, understand why he is agitated, and do something to calm him down – even if you have to oppose him tenderly but resolutely.

When you get this kind of detachment from your mind, you can look at its workings much as a watchmaker looks at the inside of a watch. When a watch is going too fast, the watchmaker doesn't throw it away. He opens it, loosens a wire or screw, and gets the machinery to go a little slower.

I had a friend who was very good at this. I used to be amazed when she would put on her magnifying glass, open my watch, look at what was hidden behind the case, and then make a few little adjustments so that the watch kept perfect time.

Similarly, after years of training, I have learned to do this with my mind. I can look at it with detachment, open it up, and see what is going on. It's a very interesting spectacle. If you know how to open your mind at the back like this, you will see to your amazement that your mind is not you; it is a process.

This is such a simple statement, but it may take a lifetime to understand and practice it. You can look inside your mind and see for yourself that in order to get angry, your mind has to speed up. To hold onto a resentment, thoughts have to keep racing around. You can actually observe the process by which the mind speeds up, and then you are able to slow it down and set it right. It means that you are not an angry person or a resentful person; you simply have a watch that goes too fast, which can be adjusted.

Once you have gained this marvelous skill of looking at your mind with detachment, you will be able to set the speed of the mind at the rate you like. You will gain the capacity, when anger comes, to slow it down and to turn it into compassion. This simple adjustment in the speed of thought is actually all that is required to transform the explosive energy of anger into the deep reserves of power that is compassion.

★

If you have been practicing meditation sincerely and

systematically, the day has to come when you enter the still center within. Then you don't hear the cars on the road outside or the music next door. All your attention is focused within, and your mind slows down almost to a crawl.

This reminds me of a story I heard about Lyndon Johnson. In the course of campaigning, it is said, he was telling some small farmers that he understood their needs because he was a rancher himself.

One man asked, "How big is your spread?"

"It's big," Johnson replied in his best Texan manner. "I get in my car in the morning, and it's sunset before I cross my own property line."

Like most farmers, this man knew politicians. "Yeah," he said, "I had that kind of car once too."

That kind of car may not be the best for inspecting a Texas ranch, but that kind of mind is excellent. Only when the mind isn't speeding can we see that there is actually an interval between one thought and another – an interval in which there is actually no thought going on at all.

This state of "no mind" is so beneficial to body and mind, so revealing of the nature of life, that once you discover it you become unshakably secure. You know that even if something terribly upsetting happens – a bereavement, a dismissal from your job, an attack, a financial loss – you have only to enter that interval where there is no thought and rest there. You can sit down for meditation with no movement in the mind and come back refreshed, renewed, and whole.

That is why the Buddha says, "Not your parents, not your partner, not your best friends can bring you such peace as a well-trained mind." The Bible calls it "the peace that passeth all understanding." You alone can find this peace for yourself, for it lies in the depths of your own consciousness. All of us are human enough to want to be comforted, and we often feel we need consolation from others. But the Buddha reminds us that although others can wipe away our tears and comfort us, who can heal the wounds of the mind? How can anyone reach the pain inside? There we have to be our own healer; no one else can do this for us.

★

This gap of stillness between one thought and another is our safety. While driving, I am told, there should be one car length between cars for every ten miles per hour of speed. When you are going fifty miles per hour, for example, safe driving demands that you maintain the distance of five car lengths between your car and the car in front.

Similarly, I would say, we can learn not to let one thought tailgate another. Tailgating thoughts are a danger signal. People who are prone to anger – or to fear, or greed, or hostility – allow no distance between one thought and another, between one emotional reaction and the next. Their anger seems continuous – just one anger car after another, bumping into each other on a fast, crowded highway.

When a person is like this, we are likely to say, "Better not go near him! He's an angry person." Prudently, we keep our distance. But I don't avoid angry people. In fact, I am often able to help them because I don't see anger as a continuous phenomenon. I see it as little bursts of anger: one burst, then another, then a third, a fourth, a fifth. When you are getting angry, if you could only slow your mind down a little, you would be able to see that between one angry thought and the next there is actually no connection at all. That is one reason the mantram can be of such help. When you repeat the mantram when you are angry, you are inserting it between angry thoughts and pushing them apart. The mantram acts like a traffic cop: "Okay, break it up!" Your thoughts slow down, and you begin to see things more clearly and understand what is the best action to take.

A person whose mind is slow lives in a wonderful world. He can cause nobody any harm; she can cause herself no harm. There is a sign in such a person's mind to slow down traffic: "Go Slow, Children Playing."

With most of us, the situation is very different. We need a sign that says, "Caution, Adults Angry." When adults are bursting out in anger, you need to be awfully careful. But when your own mind is slow, you will be calm under attack. You will be in control of your own responses. Then you will not be afraid of angry people; you will be able to face them with affection in your heart, security in your mind, and a quiet confidence that you can slow down their anger. Even a belligerent person can sense that you are remaining calm, so you not only remain free from anger yourself but help the other person to calm down too.

We are told that the mind and body are geared for either fight or flight. But there is a third alternative: we can face a difficult situation calmly, with compassion.

Mahatma Gandhi, who called himself a practical idealist, said that he wanted to live in peace not only with his friends, but with his enemies also. He knew that there were people who disliked him and opposed him, but he wanted to be able to love and respect them.

This is a sound approach to life. When you allow yourself to dislike someone, your peace is disturbed – not their peace of mind but your own. Tragically, we are bound to those people we dislike and shackled to those whom we hate.

It is essential to be able to slow down the mind enough that we don't have an automatic negative response when facing criticism. If we want sound health and unshakable security, we have to learn to be loving and calm under all circumstances. We have to learn to be as concerned about the welfare of those who dislike us as we are for those who like us. And we have to be the same whether people respect us or censure us. A fast mind cannot do these things. But when you have trained your mind, you can move into any situation, ready for anything.

★

We all need the protection of a well-trained mind. If life were always pleasant, it wouldn't matter so much if our minds were speeding out of control. But life has a way of presenting us with speed bumps. If you hit a speed bump at seventy miles per hour, you are going to be in the hospital. When life puts up speed bumps, we have to be able to slow down to get over them without injury.

Here is where you can use all the strategies I have given in the preceding chapters. When life throws up an obstacle – say, a problem that is getting unpleasant – don't swell it with your attention. Put your attention fully on your work, work hard without thinking about yourself, and repeat your mantram in your mind whenever you can to keep hold of the center of stillness you tapped in the morning's meditation. This simple strategy can keep your mind from speeding up under the pressure of any problem. At the end of the day, you will find that your problems have been reduced to a manageable size. Remember, problems have a way of swelling when we feed them with our attention; when they are starved for attention, they shrink or even go away.

These are valuable skills, which can free us not only from useless worry about today's problems but from old memories and resentments as well. Older people particularly need this skill. It is sad to listen to older people talk vividly about events that happened ten years ago – often, as the Buddha says, about how someone abused them, someone injured them, someone robbed them. In people who dwell on such thoughts, the Buddha says, hatred, anger, and resentment can never cease.

Through years of practice I have trained my mind not to dwell on those thoughts, and as a result, they don't come to me. Gandhi said that this can go to such an extent that such thoughts do not come even in our dreams.

This strategy is particularly important in safeguarding ourselves from the suffering caused by negative emotions like depression, dejection, despondency, inadequacy, and guilt.

This problem of guilt, in particular, is one of the most burdensome banes of modern life. But it is only one more of the many tricks the mind uses to get us to dwell on ourselves. You will never get bored studying your mind. It always comes up with surprises, and one of the most unpleasant of these surprises is guilt. The mind starts singing its refrain – "How terrible you were that day! You should be ashamed of yourself! Don't you feel embarrassed when you think about what you did?" And we fall in: "Oh, yes!"

At these times, the mind is only playing one of its favorite tapes. Imagine buying a new tape deck, setting it up, and arranging your speakers to get perfect sound; then you take out this old tape full of hiss and static and sit down happily to listen to the same old tired recording! Not only that, but you set it to automatically repeat itself whenever it reaches the end.

The first or second time, there may be a purpose in listening to this tape if it enables you to learn from some past mistake. But the tragedy of getting caught in a guilt complex is that we go on helplessly sitting there listening to this obnoxious, debilitating message as if to immerse ourselves in thoughts of how bad we are. When our tape deck plays what it likes, that is all we can do. But what a relief just to be able to reach over, press the Stop button, and put in a new tape – say, one of the passages we use in meditation.

★

Every human heart has a deep need to love – to be in love, really, with all of life. This is the kind of love that comes when the mind is still.

In this sense, Romeo and Juliet are in preschool as far as love goes. Men and women like Francis of Assisi and Teresa of Avila have taken their doctorates and become fully tenured professors. They are the ones who truly know what love means.

I wish I could convey to you the endless romance of this love that flows from the still mind. If you can find joy in being in love with one person, isn't the joy a millionfold greater if you can be in love with all?

When I travel on the freeways I see stickers that say, "I love my dog," "I love my cat," or "I love New York." If I were ever to put a sticker on my car, it would just say, "I love." That is our human legacy, and we claim our legacy when the mind is stilled. This is what the Bible means when it says, "Be still and know I am God."

Be still and know that we are all God's children; then you will be in love with all.

You don't know what real love is until you love all. When the mind is still, you see everybody as your own self. You see every country as your own. You will not be capable of harming anybody, even if they have harmed or hurt you; you will help even those who harm you. That is the nature of the love that flows from the hearts of people like Francis and Teresa and Gandhi.

All of us need this universal love, and all of us are looking for it – but we look for it somewhere outside. We don't know that it can be found within, at the still center within the heart.

★

When the mind is stilled, it is like crossing the timberline on a mountain peak. Mountain climbers will tell you that beyond a certain elevation no trees can grow. When the mind is stilled, no fragmentary, fraudulent thoughts can grow: no selfish urges, no resentments, no hostilities. All those who have become established in this state say on the basis of their personal experience that this is infinite joy and infinite love, for which all of us are born.

Great geniuses in fields like poetry, science, and music have experienced recurring periods of this stillness of the mind. Einstein recognized this when he said that the highest mode of knowing is the mystical. But while scientists and artists experience only fleeting glimpses of this stillness, it is men and women of God who are established in it always. They take a little of that healing stillness with them wherever they go.

In my lifetime, I have been privileged to have seen several such men and women in India. One of them, Swami Ramdas, tells us on the strength of his own experience that we can never know what real joy is until the mind is still. Until then, he says, we are simply picking up a few crumbs of pleasure and trying to convince ourselves that it is joy.

We are not here to walk about pecking at crumbs like pigeons, Ramdas says. It is our destiny to fly. Not just the fortunate few, but every one of us has been born to soar. And until we do, we can find no lasting peace anywhere. In a different simile, Ramdas tells us that "the river of life struggles through all obstacles and conditions to reach the vast and infinite ocean of existence who is God. . . . It knows no rest, no freedom, and no peace until it mingles with the waters of immortality and delights in the visions of infinity."

Similarly, Mechthild of Magdeburg, a Western mystic of the thirteenth century, described in beautiful poetry the immense benefits that flow from a mind at rest and a heart full of love. This is neither theory nor metaphysics, but a record of her own personal experience:

> Of the heavenly things God has taught me,
> I can speak but a little word,
> not more than a honey bee can carry away on its feet
>   from an overflowing jar.
> In the first choir is happiness, the highest of all gifts.
> In the second, gentleness.

In the third, loving-kindness.
In the fourth, sweetness.
In the fifth, joyfulness.
In the sixth, honorable rest.
In the seventh, riches.
In the eighth, merit.
In the ninth, fervent love.

I particularly like this phrase "honorable rest." Mechthild is being very careful about her phraseology. She says not just "rest" but "honorable rest": that is, resting at the center while contributing to life in full measure. When your mind is still, you can work hard and be active every day of your life and still be at rest, because you will not be working under the goad of personal ambition. That's the secret of Gandhi, who worked for a selfless cause fifteen hours a day seven days a week even in his seventies but never got exhausted, because, he said, "I am always at rest."

★

Many years ago our friend Mary asked Christine and me if we would like to go to Yosemite. "I think you will enjoy camping," she said. "The mountains are beautiful this time of year."

"I spent the first sixteen years of my life as a camper," I bantered, "and that's enough."

But in the end we did go with her to the beautiful Yosemite Valley.

I was expecting a wilderness, so I was astonished to

see hordes of people in a crowded campground full of transistor radios, barbecue equipment, and recreational vehicles. In fact, throughout that day we didn't see much but cars and campers. "Why come to Yosemite," I wondered, "when you can see all this in Oakland?"

But that night, when people had finally gone to sleep and the cars and radios were silent, I emerged from my meditation to hear a little brook warbling past the tent, singing its song: *Rama, Rama, Rama* . . . "Where was this brook during the day?" I wondered. "Wasn't it here then?" It had been there, of course; we simply hadn't been aware of it. People, cars, and radios had drowned its sweet voice in their racket. Only when all of this had fallen silent could we hear the gentle, soothing sound of its music.

It is the same with the mind. As long as it is blaring as usual, we cannot hear the "still, small voice" inside. Meditation is for the purpose of quietening the tumult of the mind, so that, after a long, long period, when this cacophony has been brought to an unregretted end, we hear the healing silence which has been going on within us all the time.

When we can rest our mind at will, still our mind at will, we live in a world that is one. Today, we don't see the world as it is; we see only conflict, separateness, and ceaseless change. As the Bible says, we see "as through a glass darkly," because we look through the distorting glass of our mind. We see our world through a mind fogged by anger, fear, lust, greed, and all the other negative emotions which are part of the human condition. It is William Blake, a favorite poet of mine, who says, "If the doors of perception were cleansed everything would appear as it is, infinite."

You and I, when the mind is still, see that the mountains and the seas, the forests and the rivers, the animals and the birds, the trees and the plants, all nations, all races, all men and women and children, are one. Once you see this in the silence of your heart, you will never be the same person again. You will return from this summit of spiritual awareness full of practical wisdom, passionate love, and untiring energy which you will want to use for the benefit of all.

Eight Steps

THESE ARE THE eight points of the program for effective living which I have used in my own life. It is elaborated much more fully in my book *Meditation*, which has a full chapter on each step, and in a set of four audiocassettes entitled *The Theory and Practice of Meditation*.

As a kind of review, each point is accompanied here by some of the relevant suggestions I made in preceding chapters.

1. *Slowing Down*

To guard against hurrying through the day, start the day early.

Devote half an hour every morning for meditation, or for inspirational reading and reflection. Do not let anything intrude on this most precious period of your day.

Take time for a good breakfast.

Allow yourself time to get to every engagement a little early.

Simplify your life so that you do not try to fill your time with more than you can do. Start by listing your activities. Then prune the list, striking out anything that is not truly necessary and anything that is not beneficial.

Don't try to do everything you can, or even everything you want to. Keep sight of the most important things each day, and use the mantram to remind yourself to keep coming back to them.

Allow time for all your meals. Sit down and enjoy your food with others. Repeat your mantram before you eat and eat slowly.

Don't let yourself get pressured into hurrying. Whenever you find yourself beginning to speed up during the day, repeat your mantram to help you slow down.

Cultivate patience.

Don't rush those you live and work with. Give them time; you will be giving yourself time as well.

Cultivate personal relationships in all your activities. It will help to reverse the depersonalization of our world.

Reduce the time you spend watching television.

Reduce the time you spend on activities that hurry your children. It will help them to simplify their lives and enjoy what they do, and it will give you more time for them too.

It is important not to confuse slowness with sloth,

which breeds carelessness, procrastination, and general inefficiency. In slowing down, attend meticulously to details. Give your very best even to the smallest undertaking.

2. Training Attention

Avoid doing two or more things at once, even if they seem trivial and you know you can manage it.

When you do more than one thing at a time, you are teaching your mind to be scattered. That is just the opposite of concentration, which is essential for a good performance in any field.

You are also training your mind to be divided at other times: teaching it to vacillate, to get caught in past or future, to brood on problems, to act on compulsions or on impulse, and so on.

When you read and eat at the same time, for example, part of your mind is on what you are reading and part on what you are eating. You are not getting the most from either activity.

When talking with someone, give that person your full attention.

Remember the Buddha's words: "When you are walking, walk; when you are sitting, sit. Don't wobble."

When driving, give full attention to the road. Don't listen to music or talk to your passengers; tell them you need to concentrate. Similarly, when you're a passenger, don't distract the driver.

Don't bring your work home, in your briefcase or in your mind. And don't bring the problems of home into your work.

When your attention gets caught somewhere other than here and now – for example, in some past event you can't stop dwelling on – use your mantram to get your attention free. Throw yourself into work, or go for a fast walk repeating the mantram in your mind.

Everything you do should be worthy of your full attention. If it seems worthy of only partial attention, ask yourself if it is really worth doing.

Remember that even if an activity seems trivial, you are training your mind.

3. Training the Senses

In the food we eat, the books and magazines we read, the movies we see, the television shows we watch, all of us are subject to the dictatorship of rigid personal likes and dislikes.

To free yourself from this conditioning, practice juggling with your likes and dislikes cheerfully when it is in the interests of those around you (or yourself).

Juggle with your opinions too, especially when you find that you are rigid or emotional about them. The opinions you cherish may actually not be any better than those of other people.

Practice working cheerfully with someone you think you don't like.

Don't waste time getting caught in past or future. Repeat your mantram to bring your full attention back to the present.

Choose what you eat by what is good for your body rather than by taste.

Similarly, the mind eats too, through the senses. Choose very carefully what you read and watch and listen to. Ask yourself whether it elevates or lowers your image of yourself and others.

Remember that we are what we think. What goes into your mind becomes part of what you are.

4. Putting Others First

Dwelling on yourself builds a wall between you and others.

When you find yourself dwelling on your own needs, your own wants, your own plans, your own ideas, repeat your mantram and turn your attention to the needs of others.

Practice putting the welfare of other people first, before your own. You can begin within the circle of your family and friends, where there is already a basis of love and respect on which to build.

Make a game of finding ways to do this: let the other person choose dinner for both of you, for example, or go to the film the other person wants to see.

Share activities with your children. Enjoy their enjoyment.

Don't compete in any relationship. Look for ways to complete each other instead.

When differences arise, remember that to disagree, it is not necessary to be disagreeable.

Take time to listen with complete attention and respect – there may be less to disagree about than you think.

If you have children, put their welfare first. When this means saying no – which is very important with children – it can be done with love, tenderness, and respect.

5. Spiritual Companionship

Cultivate time with people whose company elevates you.

It is especially helpful to spend time regularly with others who are basing their lives on the same spiritual values. If you are trying to follow the program presented here, association with others following the same program is invaluable. (You may write Nilgiri Press, P.O. Box 256, Tomales, California 94971, to see if there are people in your area.)

Share your times of entertainment with such people too. Relaxation is an important part of learning to slow down.

6. Spiritual Reading

The media drown us in such a low image of the human being that it is essential to remind ourselves constantly of something higher.

For this reason I recommend half an hour or so each day for reading from the scriptures and the writings of the great mystics of all religions. Just before bedtime, after evening meditation, is a particularly good time, because the thoughts you fall asleep in will be with you throughout the night.

Choose your path carefully. A good spiritual teacher lives what he or she teaches, and it is the student's responsibility to exercise sound judgment. Once you have chosen, give your teacher your full loyalty.

7. The Mantram

A mantram, or Holy Name, is a powerful spiritual formula which has the capacity to transform consciousness when it is repeated silently in the mind. There is nothing magical about this. It is simply a matter of practice, as you can verify for yourself.

Choose a mantram that appeals to you deeply from the list of those I recommend on pages 178–179. (If you are in doubt, I recommend Mahatma Gandhi's mantram, *Rama Rama*.) Once you have chosen, do not change it.

Repeat your mantram silently whenever you get the chance: while walking, while waiting, while doing mechanical chores like washing dishes, and especially when you are falling asleep. You will find that this is not mindless repetition; the mantram will help to keep you relaxed and alert.

Whenever you are angry or afraid, nervous or worried or resentful, repeat the mantram until the agitation subsides. The mantram works to steady the mind, and all these emotions are power running against you, which the mantram can harness and put to work for you.

If possible, when you are agitated, go out for a fast walk repeating your mantram in your mind. The rhythm of your footsteps will combine with the rhythm of breathing to steady the rhythm of your mind.

These and many other ways for using a mantram to deal with the problems of modern life are elaborated in my book *The Unstruck Bell*.

8. Meditation

This is the heart of my program: meditation for half an hour every morning, as early as is convenient.

Do not increase this period; if you want to meditate more, have half an hour in the evening also, preferably at the very end of the day.

Set aside a place in your home to be used only for

meditation and spiritual reading. Don't use it for any other purpose.

Sit in a straight-backed chair or on the floor with your head, neck, and spinal column erect.

Then close your eyes and begin to go slowly, in your mind, through the words of one of the passages I recommend you memorize for use in meditation. I suggest learning first the Prayer of Saint Francis of Assisi, which you will find on pages 185–186.

Do not follow any association of ideas or try to think about the passage. If you are giving your attention to each word, the meaning cannot help sinking in.

When distractions come, do not resist them, but give more attention to the words of the passage.

If your mind strays from the passage entirely, bring it back gently to the beginning and start again.

When you reach the end of the passage, you may use it again as necessary to complete your period of meditation until you have memorized others.

It is helpful to have a wide variety of positive, practical, inspiring passages for meditation. I especially recommend:

* the Twenty-third Psalm
* the Shema
* the Lord's Prayer
* the Beatitudes
* Saint Paul's "Epistle on Love" (1 Corinthians 13)

* Thomas a Kempis, *Imitation of Christ,* III.5
    ("The Wonderful Effect of Divine Love")
* The Dhammapada of the Buddha, Chapter 1
* The Bhagavad Gita, 2.54–72; 9.26–34;
    Chapter 12 ("The Way of Love"); and 18.49–73
* Ansari of Herat, "Invocations"

These and many other wonderful passages can be found in my collection *God Makes the Rivers to Flow.*

★

When this eightfold program is followed daily to the very best of one's ability, as I can testify from my own personal experience, it is possible for everyone to lead a secure, selfless life. Even a little such practice will begin to transform your life, leading to profoundly beneficial changes in yourself and in the world around you.

Index

INDEX

INDEX

INDEX